Phoebe's Sisters:
Women Leaders
in Early Christianity

Deslee Campbell

Book 1 in the Memorable Christians Series

Chapter 1

Introduction

Women in Early Christianity: that is known territory – but women leaders in Early Christianity!! Who are they?

Why is this book important?

Every book reaches a readership. Most Christians have been taught very little about Christian women in Antiquity, except for the Virgin Mary. Even what little has been taught about Mary Magdalene is probably wrong. I am forever indebted to Professor Carolyn Osiek who visited Sydney in 1994 and introduced me to the fact that women have a history: and that was fifty years after my Bachelor of Arts Modern History major. More than a century ago Jane Austin had written that history was all about wars, politics and dynastic successions and that was the history that I had learnt. Kings and their wars are handy pegs to hang chronology on but think how bland the Tudor Period would be without the story of its women and their intrigue and passion, romance and childbirth, divorce and deaths. Relationships create the fabric of human society and fifty-percent or more of any society is female. Their contribution matters and, in the Early Christian centuries, many of them were trail blazers.

There are many types of leaders and leaderships. They can be identified by the fact that they have followers: others attend to what they say, or copy what they do. This applies to women. Do others (male or female) attend to their words or follow their actions?

The women considered here were exemplary in numerous ways: their holiness and piety; their knowledge of the Scriptures, their study of Biblical languages and the writings of the earlier Christian teachers; their kindness, their hard work, their disciplined lives, their devotion to God through chastity, their disdain for money and finery, their charity to the poor and their willingness to promote the good of others rather than of themselves.

Beginning at the beginning of Christian history, with the Virgin Mary, this book considers women leaders up to the 6th century.

Chapter 2
Mary the Mother, Mary Magdalene and Mary of Clopas

The story of the women of Early Christianity begins before the beginning, even before the birth of Jesus the Christ. So with this book – it begins with Mary, especially with some intriguing new developments in Marian scholarship. It finishes with obscure women whose epitaphs are all that we know of them.

2.1: The Virgin Mary

Because this is such a vast topic only two aspects will be considered here. The first is the effects of the 2nd century infancy narrative called *The Book of James* or *The Protevangelium of James* which rivalled the nativity accounts in the gospels of Luke and Matthew, and is still highly valued in the East where it is sometimes included as an appendix to the New Testament. The second is a new perspective on the Virgin Mary proposed by Ally Kateusz in her book *Mary and Early Christian Women: Hidden Leadership* (2019).[1]

The *Book of James* makes much of celibacy: Mary was given to Joseph to care for but not to marry as he was (apparently) so old; Mary passed the usual (Jewish) 'trial by bitter waters' and so proved her innocence; the midwife Salome checked manually that her virginity was still intact after the delivery. This work incorporates many aspects from Judaism yet includes the etraordinary idea that Mary entered the Holy of Holies, but, as it not canonical, its narrative cannot be verified.

It should not surprise 21st Century readers to learn that women's history has been air-brushed out of Early Christian texts, but this is what Ally Kateusz has shown, by carefully analysing changes (omissions and deliberate alterations) to original or earlier texts. She has utilised cases where there are many examples from different centuries so that trends could be established.

Plate 2.1. Traditional house of the Virgin Mary, Ephesus. Erik Cleves Kristensen [2]

Two things in particular are shown: women's names are deliberately eliminated and replace by general terms such as 'a woman' and their stories are shortened so that they become anonymous and/or less significant. Even more importantly Ally Kateusz has shown that the old adage that 'the shortest text is the oldest text' is quite incorrect. The longest text is the original because scribes, copyists and translators of successive centuries made deliberate or accidental ommissions. In particular Kateusz follows one particular narrative of the death of the Virgin (called the Dormition) to show that, in the early centuries, Mary was a leader, evangelist and teacher in the church with higher status than Peter but that her role and status were reduced as the texts were gradually changed. The earlier Mary is a contrast to the impression that she was a submissive, obedient young woman and later a poor old widow who needed St John to care for and provide for her. Even though the earliest version is the most accurate version of the original text, however, that does not establish its verity. It may be entirely fictitious.

2.2: Mary Magdalene

The English name Mary came form the Hebrew Miriam, who was Moses' and Aaron's older sister and it was by far the most common Jewish female name in 'the Jesus period'. Mary of Magdala and Mary Clopas were two of the numerous important Marys of the gospel story.

In the gospels Mary Magdalene is mentioned twelve times, more often than most of the twelve apostles and the second female after the Virgin Mary in importance.[3] All four gospels place her at the foot of the cross with the Virgin, with whom she had a close relationship. It does seem, especially from St John's gospel-records, that Mary Magdalene had a particularly close relationship with Jesus. Jesus had cast out *"seven demons"* from her, but Mary Magdalene was not the sinful woman of Luke 7:38, but perhaps one who was delivered from psychological problems. It was Gregory the Great who, in 591 C.E., confused Mary of Bethany with the unknown sinful woman who anointed Jesus' feet and with Mary Magdalene.[4] The result was that the reputation of the faithful, zealous, apostle Mary was tarnished, until the Vatican sorted out the problem in 1969.[5]

The most notable feature of this Mary is that, if women are near Jesus she is there too: as close to Jesus as possible. Although she travelled about with a group of at least thirteen men she preserved her reputation and, except at the Garden Tomb, she was in the company of one or another woman. She was also a generous supporter of all of the disciples so she was obviously either an affluent widow or heiress, as there is no suggestion that she was a business woman.

The New Testament is silent about the issue of whether or not Jesus was married but perhaps Jesus' mother, Mary, would have liked Mary Magdalene as her daughter-in-law. After his crucifixion, when Jesus spokeher name Mary Magdalene recognised his voice and he said to her *"Do not hold onto me"* (Jn. 20:17), an indication of an unusually close relationship as it would have been inappropriate for a mere female disciple to touch the master, lest she be in menstrual uncleanness. At the empty tomb, when Mary thought she was addressing the gardener (v.15), she asked to be given Jesus' body so that she could take it away, an expectation more appropriate to a next-of-kin than of a female disciple.

In Judaism it would have been most irregular if Jesus was not married at over thirty yeas of age, given that men were expected to obey the Biblical injunction to *"be fruitful and multiply"* and Jesus' avowed intention was *"to fulfil all righteousness"* (Mat. 3:13). Based upon the Scripture, *"it is not good for man to be alone"* (Gen. 2:18, K.J.V.) marriage was an obligation for Jewish men, not an option, not to pander to those who lacked self-control. Bahat states that celibacy was forbidden in Judaism,[6] except for Nazarite vows that were permitted for one year only.[7] Samson, however, was a life-long Nazarite, as the Man of God (an angel) had commanded so it was possible, although exceptional (Jud. 13:7).

Neither Elijah nor Elisha nor John the Baptist had married and their wandering lifestyles precluded domesticity. Once Jesus' public, nomadic lifestyle began it would have become obvious, even to the Virgiin Mary, that his future would also fit the pattern of the wandering prophet.

There are probably more legends about Mary Magdalene than about any other Biblical woman. Artwork throughout the era always shows her near Christ and/or close to the Virgin Mary.

"All four evangelists mention Mary Magdalene at the foot of the cross. Her presence highlights her fidelity and special closeness to Jesus as well as her strength and endurance. While many fled, she was steadfast, along with other women".[8]

She was often depicted as a penitent prostitute and often wearing less than sufficient clothing and so becomes a vehicle for artistic imagination and the prortrayal of a woman's body more than an accurate reflection of the Biblical Magdalene.

At the Catholic Church of Ground Zero in New York there is a compelling new statue of Mary Magdalene going to the tomb carrying a spice box in each hand. Even this image probably reflects artistic license: she is barefooted, which is unlikely to have been the case as the terrain is very stony, with millions of small, gritty pebbles; her head is not veiled or covered in any way, which is improbable, her dress is not quite long enough and rather torn and ragged (at the neck, arms and hem-line) and her clothing consistes of only an under-garment but she was an affluent woman, not a beggar. Her strained face, however, seems accurate.

2.3. Mary of Clopas

Scholars are uncertain if this Mary was the wife, daughter or mother of Clopas but it is not likely that she was his mother. At the time of Jesus' Crucifixion Clopas was already a man of mature years with adult son(s) and his brother, St Joseph, had, perhaps, been deceased for a decade, or longer. A woman who was old enough to be their mother would not have been able to travel into Jerusalem, even on a donkey, and to stand at the foot of the cross for hours and be up before dawn to carry spices to the tomb. As to the other options, it would be much more appropriate for the Virgin's sister-in-law to have supported her on that sad occasion than for a woman of the younger generation to do so.

Furthermore there is no other indication that Clopas even had a daughter whereas his sons (Symeon and perhaps James and Joseph) certainly had a mother. The most economical interpretation is that Mary of Clopas was his wife.[9]

In Mark 15:47 this Mary was present at the Crucifixion and went with Mary Magdalene to see where Jesus' body was taken. In the Eastern church she is one of the ' *myrophoroi*' , the myrrh-bearers: the women who rose early on Easter Sunday morning to fulfil for the

precious Master the duty that women were expected to perform –
the anointing of the body with pounds of sweet smelling ointments/
perfumes and spices, which they had previously prepared at home.

Luke 23:56 states that the preparation was done before the
Sabbath-rest began. These women are usually depicted in art as being
three in number,[10] but, by combining various gospel narratives five
can be identified: Joanna, Mary Clopas, Mary Magdalene, the Virgin
Mary and Salome (called the mother of Zebedee's sons in Mat. 2:36).
There were also *"others with them"* (Lk. 24:10). Luke 24:10 states that
a certain Mary, the mother of James, both witnessed the Crucifixion
and came to the tomb with spices once the Sabbath was over. Elsewhere
this woman is called the mother of James and Joseph (Mt. 27:55) so it
was not essential for all of one's sons to be listed and perhaps Symeon
was an even younger son (if Clopas and Cleopas are the same man,
as many ancient authorities accept).[11] James may have been called 'the
less' (as in Mk. 15:40) because he was short of stature or younger than
his relatives, James-ben-Joseph and James-ben-Zebedee. Even in Jordan
today, when a mother has her first son, his name becomes her identity.
[I was called 'mother of David'].

Pause to consider this close-knit group of women. Nicodemus had
brought a humdred pounds weight of myrrh and aloes which were used
at the time of burial (Jn. 19:39-40). We are not told who provided the
spices for the women but all three synoptic gospels record that spices
and ointments/perfumes were used, perhaps not as much as had been
used at the entombment but in the earliest art-work these women were
depicted carrying little vials, but that was only a token of the quantity
they would have carried.

We can imagine a large group of presumably emotionally and
physically exhausted women, all busy in a small kitchen, weeping and
fearful, measuring, pouring, pounding, stirring and packaging,
determined to perform this last difficult and tragic service for their
beloved Jesus, hurring to get the job done before the Sabbath rest

began. This was the easy part, the task would not be completed for many hours of tension and tears. How difficult were the long hours of enforced rest and the two nights of waiting? The hardest part of their task was still ahead of them. They would have to enter the tomb, unwrap the Lord's battered, dead corpse and perform the customary rituals of love and devotion. They were obviously rehearsing it is as they walked along as they asked each other "*who will roll the stone away from the entrance of the tomb?*" (Mk. 16:3).

We know most about Mary Magdalene's responses to the resurrection: can we imagine those of Mary Clopas?

Mary-Clopas features in the gospel-story (including in John 19:25) as a caring, dedicated and helpful woman who entered the story at the time of greatest crisis in order to support the family. She is portrayed as a quiet model of godly womanhood. Her story was mentioned only briefly but her husband and her son(s) were key members of Jesus' extended family and vital to the early church so she, herself, would have been integral to all of their doings.

Chapter 3
Phoebe the Scroll Carrier and her 'Sisters'

3.1. Phoebe

Phoebe attracted greater praise from St Paul than any other women, for her work and leadership: "I commend to you our sister Phoebe a servant *(deaconess, messenger or minister)* of the church at Cenchreae. I ask you to receive her in the Lord in a way worthy of the saints and to give her any help she may need from you, for she has been a great help to many people, including me" *(Rom. 16:1-2).*

Here, in Romans 16:1-2, Phoebe is called a *'diakonos'* (deacon, minister or servant) of her church.[12] She needed hospitality in Rome because she was visiting the church there to personally present the *Epistle to the Romans*, which Paul had entrusted to her for safe delivery.[13] This was a challenging task as the cumbersome, rolled papyrus scroll was about five meters long[14] and she was responsible for it. Her journey included a dangerous voyage in the Mediterranean Sea: around the southern tips of Greece and across to the heel of Italy, around the toe and North, up the coast to the Porto. This voyage may have taken a week, rather than days. Presumably Phoebe did not travel alone, but perhaps she took a maidservant along: someone of sufficiently low status that she did not have to be mentioned.

Phoebe's first point of contact in Rome would have been Priscilla/Prisca and Aquila, who are mentioned first in Romans 16, and whose house-church is later mentioned in I Cor. 16:19. This couple would have had copies of the letter made and paid the fee for that service (which cost about six weeks wages of a day labourer, per copy)[15] and then have gathered a large assembly to hear Phoebe read the letter aloud in the meeting(s) and then interpret it.

Because Paul's letter was written in *scriptio continua* (without breaks and punctuation) he would have coached Phoebe on the correct oral presentation[16] and no one else would have been able to do this.

Phoebe would also have answered the recipients' questions and given information both about Paul and, later, back to him about the letter's reception in Rome. This was perhaps the most important public speaking to have taken place in the Roman church, until Paul arrived in person: and Paul did not hesitate to entrust it to a woman.

It is quite probable that Prisca and Aquila also had a copy made for themselvers and that they took it to Ephesus when they moved there and ran a house-church there (II Tim. 4:19 and I Cor. 16:19). Such a prized letter would have been happily received by the church in Ephesus, enhancing its teaching. Paul also requested that letters be shared between congregations (Col. 4:16).

Based upon Terry Wilder's analysis of five non-Christian authors' accounts of letter-couriers in the Roman world and two Jewish examples from Josephus, *diakonoi* (couriers/messengers) also gave verbal reports and 'fleshed-out' the written message.[17] Another task of a letter-courier was to encourage the believers, as Tychicus did when he carried four of Paul's letters: those to Ephesus, Colosse, to Philemon and Laodicea. Paul called Tychicus a *diakonos* (translated deacon, minister or servant but equally a herald or official messenger).[18] The texts about Tychicus elaborate on the task of the letter-carrier (Eph. 6:21 and Col. 4:7-8, Philemon 10, 12).

"Tychicus will tell you all the news about me .... that he may encourage your hearts" (Col. 4:7a and 8b).

"Tychicus, the dear brother and faithful servant in the Lord, will tell you everything, so that you also may know how I am and what I am doing. I am sending him to you for this very purpose, that you may know how we are, and that he may encourage you" (Eph. 6:21-22).

If Phoebe was a "herald" or "official messenger" when she was at home in Cenchreae, whose herald was she? Surely the King of Kings. A ' *diakonos*' was not a 'church mouse' who was required to keep silent in the curch.

On his second missionary journey Paul had visited Corinth's port city, Cenchreae where he (mysteriously) had his hair cut in connection with a vow (Acts 18:18). Here he met Phoebe, the female deacon or deaconess (Rom. 16:1-2).[19] A *diakonos* held an official position in the ministry, Phoebe was also affluent and so was a patroness (Rom. 16:1-2) of the house-church in her home at Cenchreae. She was a business-woman who probably travelled to Rome for this purpose and either volunteered or was asked to transport the scroll: a leather-wrapped five-metre-long vellum or parchment scroll.

3.2. *Phoebe's 'Sisters' in Rome*

The women Paul names in this lengthy epistle really were Phoebe's sisters in that she would have met them all and related to them because Paul knew of them and he had met some of them earlier (such as his 'mother' who was the mother of his friend, Rufus).[20] If Phoebe had previously been to Rome, or would be returning for business purposes, it was important that she make personal contact with all of the leading women of the Roman church.

Because the scroll Phoebe was bringing to their church mentions these men and women by name Prisca and Aquila would have made sure that all of the named recipients attended the letter-reading. Surely they did so with eager anticipation and surely they appreciated Phoebe's efforts. Paul's letter asked the congregation(s) to meet Phoebe's needs but Prisca and Aquila would have made sure that she lacked nothing.

Let us pause the narrative for a moment and consider these Roman Christians, some of whom were among Paul's closest friends. Four named people were nominated as Paul's 'beloved friends' or 'dear friends': Epenetus, Ampliatus, Stachys and a woman named Persis.[21] Also, Urbane was Paul's helper, Apelles was *"approved of Christ"* (16:9-10) and Epaenetus was the first convert in Achaia/Corinth (v.5). Herodion and Andronicus and Junia were Paul's relatives (or perhaps

fellow Jews) (v.7) as were Jason and Sosipater who travelled with him
(v.21). The Roman church must have been large because of the large
numbers of both women and men whom Paul named in Romans
Chapter 16.

The named women are an interesting group. Paul clearly knew
Mary, *"who bestowed much labour on us"* (v. 6) and of course his relative
or kinswoman the aforementioned Junia (v. 7), who will be discussed
below. Two women, Euodia and Syntyche, attracted praise from Paul
who said, *"they laboured with me in the gospel"* (Phil. 4:2).

Although Paul did not found the Church in Rome he had excellent
intelligence on it. The Christian women there were remarkably
important and numerous and because they were meant to be among
the recipients of his *Epistle to the Romans*, Paul greeted twelve female
leaders of the Roman church by name: those mentioned above as well
as Tryphaena, Tryphosa and Persis, who were his co-workers, and also
Julia, Olympas, the mother of Rufus who was a mother to Paul also,
and Nereus's sister.[22] One of those co-workers was Junia, *"outstanding
among the apostles"* (Rom. 16:7) who was probably married to
Andronicus, both perhaps distant relatives of Paul and whose
preaching engagements landed them in prison with Paul (as
Aristarchus had also been at one point, Col. 4:10).[23] The naming of
Junia as an 'outstanding apostle' so disturbed male heirarchs that an 's'
was added to her name, to turn her into a man and so continued the
fiction that women had never had any clerical or heirarchical roles.

Phoebe attracted the highest praise: even greater praise from Paul
than other women, for her work and leadership. She would have
enjoyed her success at having successfully accomplished the task Paul
had given her and to have met her many Roman 'sisters in the Lord',
who were obviously important to Paul as he commended them in this
epistle for their sterling work. Perhaps he had spoken warmly to her
about them, so that she felt she already knew them.

Chapter 4

Perpetua, Felicitas and Thekla

This chapter considers the lives and influence of three very different women who were accepted as saints in the early centuries of Christianity.

Perpetua and Felicitas were martyred together in Carthage in the very early 3rd century, even before they had been baptised and Thekla's narrative recounts several unsuccessful but violent attempts to make her a martyr, to recant, to decide not to be a Christian, but to remain a virgin. Each woman's narrative inspires a different kind of woman: Felicitas inspires the timid young mother, Thekla the dedicated virgin who wants to achieve great things for God and Perpetua the affluent matron from the upper echelons of society. All three varieties of woman were plentiful in the Early Church.

Plate 4.1. Martyrs Perpetua and Felicitas, Archbishop's Chapel, Ravenna.
Public domain.

4.1. Perpetua and Felicitas

The martyrs, Felicitas and Vibia Perpetua, are depicted in the 6th-century mosaic from the Archbishop's Chapel in Ravenna (Plate 4.2). These two young mothers were martyred in Carthage on March 7, 203, under Septimus Severus.[24]

Perpetua is depicted bejewelled and royally dressed[25] but Felicitas is shown plainly dressed, like an ascetic or nun, which she was not. The autobiographical text '*The Passion of St. Perpetua*', indicates that the difference between these two women was social class: Felicitas was a slave and Perpetua was her friend and probably her mistress.[26] These two women belonged to a small group of recent converts who were being taught prior to their baptism (that is, they were catechumen). They would be baptised in their own blood. Their instructor was the priest, Saturus, who died with them. Others of their male companions were Saturninus, Secundulus and Revocatus, who was probably married to Felicitas and/or was the father of the newly-born child.[27] The baby was miraculously delivered early so that Felicitas could receive her crown of martyrdom on the same day as her friends. She had prayed for this miracle as she did not want to have to die alone, later. What is unique about the story of Perpetual and Felicitas is that Perpetua and Saturus wrote an account of their experiences in the first-person, which was completed after their deaths by a redactor who wrote in the third-person. Perhaps this was Tertullian.[28] This rare written testimony (a unique women's voice) is generally accepted as genuine.

4.2. St Thekla

At times Thekla's popularity even rivalled that of the Virgin Mary(29) although the state of her shrine inTurkey suggests that her popularity has waned considerably. Her story may have been based upon a local girl called Thecla/Thekla but her very existence is now doubted; except as mythology spiced with exaggerated miracles.

Thekla's tradition was generated in the 2nd century by an apocryphal work called '*The Acts of Paul and Thekla*' which was widely read in Antiquity and had a profound influence on both men and women.[30] Keepsakes carried away from her shrine by pilgrims are numerous and were widely dispersed, demonstrating her popularity with ordinary people. Even a theologian as great as the Cappadocian Father, St Gregory Nazianzus, spent time at her shrine.

Plate 4.1. Remains of Holy Thekla's shrine in Turkey. Public domain.

Her story, in summary, shows Thekla as a disciple of St Paul who was transfixed by his teachings, because of which she rejeced her fiancé in favour of chastity. Unsuccessful attempts were made to burn her to death and to feed her to wild animals but she rejoined Paul and travelled around with him before being sent out by to evangelise, teach and establish churches for the rest of her life, although she had to dress as a man for her own protection. Her example was a challenge to emerging male authority as she was an apostle as well as a teacher and evangelist, which apparently contradicted Paul's canonical teachings so that women were confronted by a dilemma: which teaching should they follow?

Because Thekla's tradition was not bolstered by any mention of her in the New Testament her cult was not difficult for the Western Church to suppress, especially considering that the apostle Junia was easily dispatched by turning her into a man named Junias.[31] Thekla continued to be influential in the East and many images of her were created in the 5th or 6th centuries including on lamps and flasks(32) and the item in Plate 4.3. A functioning shrine and a monastery still exist in Syria.

Plate 4.2. Fresco of Paul and Thecla from 6th century, Public domain.

The image in Plate 4.2 is revealing.[33] It demonstrates what became of Thekla. While Paul's image has not been damaged Thekla eyes and right hand raised in blessing have been deliberately erased. "*The woman is blinded and silenced*".[34]

What really mattered was not Thekla's existence but that her tradition was believed and followed.

Pederson lists an impressive array of 4th century churchmen who accepted her historicity.[35] Her life-style was copied. It fitted well with the Gnostic tendency towards renunciation of the material world (the body, food, bathing, sleep, sexuality, recreation and soft bedding) and with emerging trends towards asceticism. Indeed it fed that trend.

In the *Acts of Paul and Thekla* Paul was said to have preached the Beatitudes of the gospels but augmented them with extra promises, such as: *"Blesssed are they that possess their wives as though they had them not, for they shall inherit God"*.[36] *"Blessed are they that keep the flesh chaste, for they shall become the temple of God"*.[37] In short, virginity and abstenance within marriage were the only paths to Heaven: *"ye have no redemption otherwise, except ye continue chaste, and defile not the flesh but keep it pure"*.[38]

Plate 4.3. Image of Thekla. Public domain.

It is not surprising that Thekla's cult flourished. Eternal salvation was easily obtained if one remained a virgin, moreover it was so much more pleasant to accept beautiful, young Thekla's miraculous survival than the dreadful stories about martyrdoms like those of Perpetua, Felicitas and their male companions, Revocatus and Secundus, Saturnus, Saturninus and Secundus.[39]

Thekla's was the palatable narrative and the palatable teaching that all Christians preferred to hear. Cohick and Hughes read Thekla's legacy as maleable. Being able to both reflect and influence the church and the individual Christian (male or female) she is a constantly changing metaphor. They suggest that her anonymity is her strength as she morphs into another reality as needed.[40] This perhaps works at the subconscious level but a more economic explanation is that Thekla was embraced because hers was a 'feel good story' with just enough drama, threat, gore and sexuality to make an interesting story but with a happy core.

Chapter 5

Early House Church Leaders

5.1. Women's Leadership of House Churches

Some men led house-churches. Examples include Philemon in Colossae (Phil. 2) and Stephanas in Corinth, whose family members were converted first and were baptised by Paul (I Cor.1:16). When others became converts they then "*devoted themselves to the service of the saints*" (I Cor.16:15).[41] Gaius and his household were converted in Corinth and baptised by Paul. A church met in this house and Paul resided there on his third visit to Corinth (Rom.16:23).[42]

Luke, the writer of Acts, particularly notes when women, especially wealthy or prominent women, joined or led Paul's church-plants. These women included Lydia in Philippi (Acts 16:14); in Thessalonica more than a few prominent women (17:4); in Beroea many prominent Greek women (17:12); in Athens, a woman named Damaris and others (17:34) and in Corinth, Priscilla (18:2; 18:18, 19).

While ever house-churches were used, from the time of Paul to Constantine, numerous women ran the churches that met in their homes.

Priscilla and Aquila opened their home for house-church meetings, in Rome (Rom 16:5), in Corinth (I Cor.16:19) and probably in Ephesus where Timothy was also ministering (II Tim. 4:19; Acts 18:18-19). As noted, Phoebe, a *diakonos* (a female deacon, minister, servant or messenger) and also an affluent patroness (Rom. 16:1-2) ran a house-church at Cenchreae, near Corinth, as also Nympha did in Colosse or Laodicea (Col. 4:15) and Lydia in Thyatira (Acts 16:40).

Philemon (alone, or as one of two male and one female leaders) ran a house church at Colosse (Philemon 2). Perhaps the leader Apphia was Philemon's wife, or his sister, or his mother: in any case she would have been the hostess of that church.[43]

It was not unusual for widows to own the family home; as did Peter's mother-in-law in Capernaeum. A house-church met in the home of John-Mark's mother, Mary, in Jerusalem, a lady who was sufficiently wealthy to have a large house with a courtyard and a maid (a slave-woman named Rhoda)[44] (Acts 12:12ff).[45]

The hospitality of house-churches made possible the Christian worship, common meals and courage-sustaining fellowship of the group. *"The Christian movement really rooted in these homes"*[46] but small intimate house-churches gave way to large public buildings after percutions ceased and Christianity gradually became the accepted religion of the Roman Empire.

5.2. Why Church met in Houses

From 111-113 C.E. in the East the Emperor Trajan's ban on assemblies was rigorously implemented. As the Dura house-church functioned later than this (c.235-256/7) baptisms at Dura-Europos may have been held at the same time as an Agape meal, at least during the first fourteen years of the life of this house-church. Calm was short-lived as persecution began in January 250 after Fabian, Bishop of Rome, was executed. During the short but dangerous reign of Decius (249-251 C.E.) baptisms would have been secretive. The Decian persecution was severe and included the atrocities of forcing Christians to taste the sacrifices, to curse Christ and to prove their compliance by carrying a signed certificate around their neck.[47]

The destruction of Christian buildings applied particularly within Israel,[48] but if Christians met in private homes it was in secretive and private space. In the earliest days, when congregations met in house-churches, women were at liberty to dress, behave and take roles that were not permitted to them once public churches became the norm.

5.3. Rhoda, Mary and her son John Mark

As soon as Peter was miraculously released from prison he went straight to the home of Mary and John-Mark.[49] Peter was probably the leader of this group which was in earnest prayer for him: so it is not surprising that Rhoda and Peter knew each other well. Rhoda even recognised his voice and was joyful and it is easy to believe that she was a Christian, not just a slave. She began life as a gentile as Jews were forbidden to enslave other Jews and she may first have converted to Judaism as it customary for Jews to convert their slaves. It was relatively easy for women slaves to accept conversion as female conversion only required immersion and an offering, or donation, whereas male conversion to Judaism required circumcision.

Mary's son, Johannes-Marcus (John-Mark) had been provided with a good education and probably understood the Scriptures (the *Tanakh*) in Hebrew and also spoke Greek, Aramaic and some Latin. John-Mark grew up under Peter's teachings and he apparently kept in close contact with Peter as, in Rome, he became Peter's scribe and/or translator. Then, later, he attempted to record everything that he had heard from Peter, which resulted in the canonical Gospel According to St Mark.[50] Awareness of the history between the lad and the master helps to establish the reliability of this gospel. In Rome there were many literate people, including Jews, but probably few who also spoke Aramaic and also understood Biblical Hebrew. Because Mary could afford it, John-Mark received an education and so was able to become St Peter's scribe and/or translator, which resulted in St Mark's Gospel.

Women church-leaders would have been literate or have worked very closely with literate husbands or perhaps literate slaves.[51] Literacy was generally not rare among Jews but difficult in Rome' where the population was bi-lingual until the 4th century and Roman and Greek scripts were very different,[52] not to mention the Hebrew which many Jews knew. Rome was a large city and the centre of the Empire for diplomacy, communications, law, finance, the Roman cult, commerce, education, trading, literature, entertainment, the military machine and government so a large workforce that was literate in Latin, the language of administration, was required. Perhaps one third of Rome's population had at least basic literacy.[53]

5.4. Dura-Europos: the *domus eklesia*

Unfortunately we do not have material remains of the Pauline house-churches but we do have evidence of a house-church (converted from a villa between 232 and 265 C.E.)[54] found in Dura-Europos on the border between the Roman and Parthian empires. It was excavated under Carl Kraeling in the 1970s.

This house-church, built within a villa at Dura-Europos was destroyed, not by imperial command but for practical reasons, to enhance the city's defenses. This house-church was short-lived.

The ground floor of the two-storey villa had a *triclinium* that was converted into the meeting hall of a house-church or *domus eklesia* as the ground floor was given entirely for Christian use.[55] In the floor plan in Plate 5.1 entry (at E) was by way of the vestibule (front right on the floor plan). The ground floor had six main elements: a large, tiled central courtyard (1) and two porticos (2 and 3), a service room or vestry (5), a baptistery (6), and a large meeting room (4) (which was originally two rooms). This enlarged room was about five by sixteen metres and, after it was altered, it potentially seated 60 to 70 people, if they sat in rows, facing the rectangular bema.[56] There was a staircase between the baptistery and the entry-porch, which led upstairs to the living-quarters. Other stairs went down to a basement from one corner of portico 2 (its position is not shown). The position of the bema (in 4) suggests that listening to readings and sermons would have been the main activities.

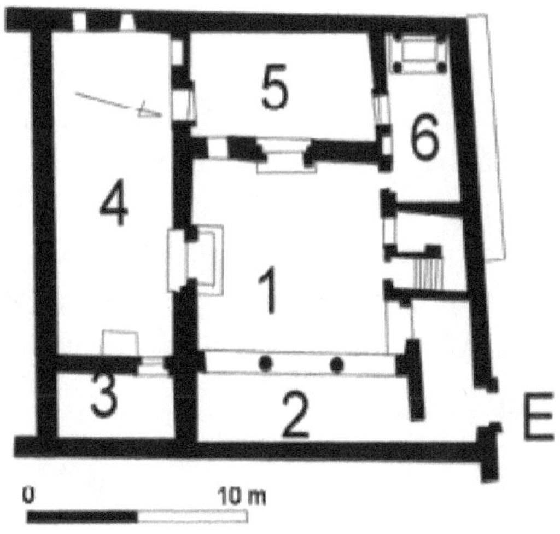

Plate 5.1. See footnote 55. House-church at Dura-Europos. By Udimus.

The steps that went up to the meeting hall (4) were used most frequently but, if adults or children were to be baptised, they would have used the steps up to the vestry (5) where they waited and then disrobed while the water was being organised and everyone assembled. There was only enough space in the baptistery for a few people: perhaps only the clergy, the candidate and sponsors or God-parents. The font is not large enough for full immersion so adult candidates probably sat in it so that water could be poured three times over the head (in the name of the Father, Son and Holy Spirit). Anointing[57] and salting probably also occurred. The colour-plate below shows an amphora placed within an arched niche to the right of the tub/font, which is quite consistent with the need to pour water upon the head.

5.5. The Baptistery at Dura-Europos

The owners (or perhaps only a widow) lived upstairs and probably ran the house-church at Dura, carefully vetting whoever came in. As noted, this villa contained a small internal baptistery, which has become famous because of its early but secure mid-3rd-century date.

There was a river nearby but open-air baptisms would have been unwise; or even quite dangerous.

The artwork of this Christian baptistery and of its contemporary, the lavishly decorated synagogue situated nearby, provide a glimpse of early religious painting. In the baptistry: the Good Shepherd is central, above the font, and other, much-damaged, painted scenes are arranged in two registers. They include the Maries (myrrh-bearers) going to the tomb on Easter morning (or the wise virgins), the paralytic carrying his bed, Jesus walking on water, Adam and Eve, the woman at the well and perhaps David and Goliath.[58]

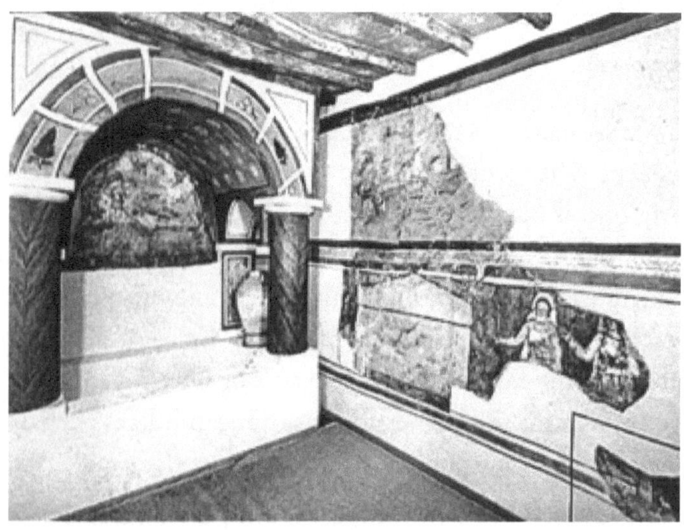

Plate 5.2. Dura-Europos baptistry in Yale University. Public domain.

5.6. The DuraEuropos Synagogue

Nearby, the walls of the Dura Synagogue were lavishly covered with complex narrative scenes from the Hebrew Scriptures[59] but the same artist, Siseos, wrote his name in both the baptistery and in the central niche of the synagogue[60] an intriguing glimpse into contact between the two groups. Siseos was acceptable to both groups and he knew the stories from both Testaments.

Although the paint work of the baptistery is too degraded to make a good comparison between them the art-work at Dura-Europos was much more competent than that of the non-figurative work on the interior walls of a contemporary chapel at Legio, in Israel. Although his name is virtually unknown, a great debt of gratitude is owed to Siseos by Jews and Christians alike.

5.7. Discussion

The apostolic period was a golden age for Spirit-led, warm, intimate fellowship. Both men and women fulfilled ministry opportunities as needed, before a controlling, clerical, hierarchy developed. Even though Temple worship continued until 70 C.E., and Jesus' disciples continued to worship there (Acts 2:46-7) private worship of both God and Jesus was possible within the house-church.[61] Such fellowship was sustaining and encouraging. The existence of house churches is known from the New Testament and St Paul established them in the Diaspora around key people of status and/or leadership potential who owned substantial homes. Such leaders were often married couples or women.

Because private domestic space was the female domain women were active in both hospitality and leadership in house-churches. A major issue developed later. "*Public space was male space*"[62] but was the basillica-church (and indeed the synagogue) public or private space?

Discord between groups apparently did develop, for example in Corinth and Galatia, but few real facts are known. According to the epistle known as *I Clement* there was 'trouble in Corinth' - a sedition by dissidents who deposed some of the presbyters. Filson opines that the trouble in Corinth resulted from house-churches which disagreed and conflicted with one another. This is based upon the leadership each claimed. Indeed Paul had been very concerned by a party spirit: 'I follow Paul' and 'I follow Apollos' (I Cor 3:3) and v. 22 where Cephas is mentioned, along with the other heroes. These distinctions destroyed the harmony which Paul meant them to enjoy.[63]

These were dangerous times and intermittent suffering did occur but homely gatherings overseen by hostesses and hosts would have been supportive. They would have evoked Jesus' meals with his chosen disciples, continuing until the Constantinian peace permanently changed the face of *Ecclesia*.

5.8. Women's Leadership: According to Tertullian

Before the Constantinian peace but more than a century after Paul's Epistles were penned, Tertullian, (c.180-c.220), in North Africa, regarded the church, like the marketplace, not as a private home but as a public space.[64] He railed against professed virgins who took advantage of their right, as single women, not to wear a veil in church and against women who taught and baptised when they should "*keep silence*" as St Paul said (I Cor. 14:34).[65] Those were not Tertullian's only criticism of females: he also condemned women who wore mascara and rouge and used face creams to lighten their skin and who wore gold and silver jewellery, precious stones, and pearls.[66]

Tertullian wrote in Latin, not Greek: the first Christian theologian to do so.[67] Therefore he greatly influenced the Western church, despite later being a Montanist. Tertullian's women were to be dowdy, silent and to stay in the home[68] and they certainly were not expected to participate actively in church services. In a century and a half, women had slipped from being presbyters and deacons to (in Tertullian's opinion) being sidelined and silenced.[69]

Tertullian's influence greatly contributed to the reduced role and status of women in the Western Church compared with that of the East. At the same time that he was sounding out against women's leadership male writers were recording that Mother Mary had done those very things, including baptising people.

5.9 Conclusions

The church heirarchical system (which was modelled upon the Jewish Temple) did not develop immediately and it began with deacons who did not have a spiritual role: that was retained by the apostles. Although as Judaeo-Christians they continued to frequent the Temple, speaking about Jesus and his worship had to remain private. Those who had large homes naturally became involved in house-meetings and hospitality and were as likely to be women as men. The earliest congregations were egalitarian and very close knit.

Chapter 6

Marcella of Rome

6.1. St Marcella of Rome (325-410 CE)

Although Marcella is a saint to the Eastern and Roman Catholic Churches she is not well known but she was everything that was considered good in holy women of the 4th century: a nun, an abbess, an ascetic, a woman of prayer and the Scriptures, a teacher, an altruist, a mother figure and a martyr.

Marcella's mother was Albina, her sister was Asella and her father was of high rank. They had a palatial home on the Aventine Hill in Rome where they hosted some notable houseguests in the 340s including the Egyptian Patriarch, St Athanasius of Alexandria (296-373). He gave Marcella a copy of his *Life of St Anthony* (St Anthony/Antony being the founder of Egyptian monasticism), which she read and treasured.

When Marcella's husband died after seven months of marriage she naturally looked to the life that St Anthony exemplified and turned her home into a monastery and was the first woman of high rank in Rome to embrace monastic life, behaving like a pauper in plain sight and giving away her wealth.

As an independent, aristocratic, educated, wealthy woman Marcella could mix in the highest circles. She had worn silk garments but she chose humility and poverty in order to serve the poor: she and her followers wore simple brown robes and were called the Brown Shirt Society.[70] Many Christians, including Jerome for three years, St Paula, her daughters Ss Eustochium and Blaesilla, and St Melania the Elder, came under Marcella's sway and they all embraced asceticism and the monastic way of life. Marcella also encouraged a love of and serious study of the Scriptures, including in their original languages: Hebrew and Greek, which they all learnt with various degrees of success: Paula most successfully.

Once Jerome was no longer available, having been exiled from Rome, the Pope (Anastasius I) and many others consulted Marcella for sage advice and Scriptural interpretations.[71]

Marcella contributed to the 'Origenist controversy' by collecting witness statements about the damage that Origen's theories had caused to Christians and, according to Jerome, she virtually single-handedly dismantled their errors.[72]

At the age of 85, Marcella was assaulted by the Gothic invaders of Rome under Alaric in 410 and died the next day.[73]

Two years after Marcella's death her former pupil, St Jerome, write *Letter* 127 of consolation to St Principia, her spiritual daughter. He had lived in Marcella's home for three years and loved her as a mother. He extolled Marcella's personal virtues and efforts to save the Church in Rome from the negative effects of the teachings of Origen, who had been martyred in 254, especially his doctrines of the *"pre-existence of the soul"* and the *"restoration of all things"* (Universalism). These were seen as minimising or denying the Incarnation and disparaging the body in favour of the spirit (as the Greeks tended to do). Late in the 4th century controversy raged about his divergent beliefs, especially his Universalism.

Origen's theology seems to have been favoured by Rufinus of Aquilia, who, like Jerome, translated Origen's *On First Principles* so that each one accused the other of being a worse heretic than himself. Marcella's contribution to the 'Origenist controversy' was to collect witness statements about the damage that these theories had caused to Christians and, according to Jerome, she virtually single-handedly dismantled the errors of Origen's views.

6.2. Conclusions

At the age of 85 years St Marcella was brutally treated by the army of Alaric during their invasion of Rome in 410 AD and soon died of her wounds in the arms of her spiritual daughter, St Principia.

Marcella was central to the faith of numerous Christians, even Pope St Damasus I and Pope Anastasius. She was probably the first Christian woman to engage in serious study of Biblical languages so as to accurately translate them and apparently the founder of female monasticism in the West.

St Jerome called her *"the glory of her native Rome"* (Ep. 127.1.) and her relative, Paulinus of Nola said of her, *"what a woman she is, if one can call so virile a Christian a woman"* (*Ep.* 29 5-6).

Chapter 7

Western Women: St Monica

7.1. St Monica (c.331-387 CE)

St Monica, a Berber from Africa, was the widow of Patricius, a pagan man of high status who was baptised in old age.74 Married life in Tagaste (Algeria) had been particularly difficult to endure as Patricius was short-tempered but as a Christian Monica learnt patience, long-suffering, wisdom and devotion in the school of life.

There were three children: Augustine (354-430), his brother, Navigius and one sister, Perpetua. Monica laboured in prayer and fasting for many years, while Augustine was living a dissolute life searching for the truth in various philosophies and sects (such as Manicheanism[75] and Neo-Platonism). Augustine lived with an unnamed woman who was of a lower social class and by whom, as a nineteen year old, he had a son, Adeodatus. Monica was the grandmother of Adeodatus.

Augustine briefly taught in Rome (in 383-84) and then took a position as professor of rhetoric at the imperial court of Milan.[76] Bishop Ambrose of Milan (c.340-397) was famed as a rhetorician, which interested Augustine sufficiently to attend his church as *a careless and scornful looker-on*.[77] When Monica arrived in Milan she was delighted with Bishop Ambrose's preaching and loved him as an angel of God. As Ambrose was often unable to meet them Augustine found Simplicianus, an old rhetorician who had taught Ambrose.[78] Augustine longed to surrender to God but was held prisoner by his lusts and ambitions.[79]

Monica was sufficiently enchanted with Bishop Ambrose that she was able to overlook the fact that his edicts against eating and drinking in churches and cemeteries had curtailed her African practice of celebrating meals (*refrigeria*) at the graves of saints and martyrs. Christian praxis in the provinces often differed markedly from that in the great, sophisticated urban centres, as Augustine disclosed in his Confessions.[80]

St Monica gave Augustine the news that she had arranged a marriage for him to a suitable girl who was still too young to marry and she persuaded the reluctant Augustine to send away his son's mother, the woman whom he had loved for fifteen years. For solace, Augustine immediately took another concubine for two years.[81] "*Celibacy seemed to me a painful course,*" he wrote.[82] He advised his mother that he was no longer a Manichee, though not yet a Christian and then he discovered Neo-Platonism; which he embraced for a time.

Monica became a prayer warrior in defence of St Ambrose of Milan when the empress Justina, the Arian mother of the child Emperor, Valentinian II, began persecuting the bishop and his church. It was then, to comfort the congregation who feared for the bishop's life, that harmonious singing of psalms and hymns, as practised in the Eastern Churches, was introduced in Milan (and from there into the West).[83]

After much soul-searching and anguish, when Augustine was 33, he surrendered to God. Augustine then organised a retreat in remote Cassiciacum for eighteen weeks of rest, recreation and discussion. He gathered together his brother, Navigius, and his fourteen year old son, Adeodatus, his long-time friends, Alypius and Nebridius, and other ascetic young men, with Monica taking care of them as 'house mother' and providing wise theologian input and counsel.

Once back in Milan, at Easter 387, Augustine was baptised by Ambrose, along with Adeodatus and his friend, Alypius.[84] Augustine resigned from his position and began the return to Africa but, at the age of 55/56, Monica, having lived to see Augustine baptised, died of a fever at the Port of Ostia as they were about to sail home. A short sentence about her burial is notable as it indicates that a funeral

Eucharist was held: "*the Sacrifice of our ransom was offered for her, when now the corpse was by the grave side*".[85]

When Adeodatus, a brilliant young man of about nineteen, died in c.391, Augustine turned his home into a monastery, sold his inheritance and was ordained presbyter.[86] He was nominated by Valerius, Bishop of Hippo Regius, as his successor in 395 and consecrated bishop in 396. Augustine died in 430 during the Vandal siege after decades as a busy bishop and productive apologist against Donatism, Pelagianism and Manicheanism.[87] His *Confessions* is perhaps the first, certainly the most complete, autobiography of his era.[88]

St Monica is not usually considered a leader but when Augustine gathered a group of young men together for eighteen weeks of contemplation, discussion and study, she emerged as their leader in practical matters and in spiritual matters. So much so that Augustine wrote two books about their discussions and her wisdom, which he greatly admired: *On the Happy Life* and *On Order*.[89] Augustine, still a 'baby Christian' at the time, was amazed at the insights, practical philosophy and knowledge of the Scriptures with which she was able to teach the young men. "*For Augustine, Longevity of relationship with God and stalwart faith qualify Monica as an indispensable authority in the philosophical search for wisdom*".[90]

7.2. Conclusions

St Monica's years of difficult marital relations taught her patience, empathy and wisdom and her wayward son, Augustine, owed a great deal to her example and her guidance. Her death was typical of her life: after Augustine was baptised her job was done and she quietly slipped away.

Chapter 8

Eastern Women: Anthousa, Olympias, Nonna, the Macrinas and Emmilia

Six women, matriarchs of Christian families in the Greek speaking East, were particularly significant during this century. Between them they raised and/or taught many bishops and/or saints. All of their contributions have been downplayed by the church in favour of those whom they gave birth to, mentored, taught and cared for, and who became bishops, priests, abbots and, occasionally, abbesses. These matriarchs were learned in the ways of God, lovers of the Scriptures and, whether widows, virgins or even married women, had chosen to be consecrated to God in celibacy. They were: Anthousa, Olympias, Nonna, Macrina the Elder and Macrina the Younger and Emmilia. Virtually all of these families were interconnected by friendship and/or birth. They occasionally intermarried because they were Christians of the 'right' social class, when most people were neither, but only rarely because celibacy was valued and taught and was generally embraced by their offspring. Their families died out within a few generations (Paula, for example, had five children but only her son had any children, only one of who may have married).

Even though many of these foremost Christian women had not been born to Christian parents they embraced Jesus Christ wholeheartedly in a way that revolutionised their lives and influenced their (often pagan) husbands and determined the course of the lives of their offspring and even of their grandchildren.

8.1. St Anthousa (c.330-c.373 CE)

St Anthousa is honoured in the Orthodox tradition as the mother of a great saint. She was married to Secundus, an official of the Imperial Army in Syria. At the age of 20 when she was left a widow with a son, John, she chose not to remarry and dedicated herself to John's upbringing. She, herself, was well educated and was anxious about educating John in Antioch, a rough and large city, so she chose to home-school him, especially in the Scriptures. As John was clearly an able student Anthousa later sent him to the great scholars of the age: the pagan orator, Libanus, in Antioch, and then he studied theology under Diodore of Tarsus.

John felt so responsible for his devoted and devout mother that he was unable to follow his own calling to the monastic life so he lived with his mother under a monastic rule. St Anthousa, who sowed her life into her son, has been largely forgotten, but John, called Chrysostom, became a renowned preacher and Patriarch of Constantinople and a Doctor of the Church.[91]

8.2. St Olympias and St John Chrysostom

The story of St John Chrysostom continues after his mother's passing and is intertwined with the biography of St Olympias/ Olympiada, (c.362-409).[92]

She was the daughter of Theodosia and Seleucus the ex-count, and granddaughter of Ablabius, praetorian prefect and consul in 331.[93] Theodosia, St Olympias' mother, was the daughter of St Nonna's brother, Amfilohije (and Theodosia's brother was Bishop Amphilochius of Konya). Other authorities, however, say that St Theodosia was not Olympias's mother but her tutor, *"a most virtuous and pious women"*, and the sister of St Amphilochius.[94] If Theodosia was her mother then Olympias's great-aunt was St Nonna, a lady whom we will consider below.

At a young age Olympias had been very briefly married to Nebridius, treasurer to Emperor Theodosius the Great95 and prefect of Constantinople in 386.[96] In her early widowhood Olympias humbly but firmly refused pressure from the Emperor to accept his choice of a second husband for her as she devoted herself to the celibate life.[97] As women's celibacy was being encouraged and elevated in status and rewarded by churchmen an arranged marriage must have seemed a poor, frightening and/or distasteful option. Later Olympias was taught by Melania the Elder,[98] who, in turn, had been taught by Marcella in Rome, ladies whose lives we will also consider.

St John Chrysostom (347-407 C.E.) knew many of the personalities to be considered here: for example, Jerome spent two years in Constantinople being taught by John Chrysostom. While Chrysostom was Patriarch of Constantinople he owed much to the financial help of the extremely wealthy aristocratic widow, Olympias, who was the abbess of a monastery which she established with her great fortune beside the Great Church in Constantinople.

As an abbess, St Olympias donated to the poor, to charitable institutions and to monasteries and had been ordained a deaconess of the Great Church by her close friend, Patriarch Nectarius (381-397)[99] although she was well below the canonical age.[100] Chrysostom, as Patriarch, ordained to the diaconate three sisters of her family, who were also nuns: Elisanthia, Martyria and Palladia and also Olympias' niece, named Olympia.[101] Later Elisanthia became the abbess of this monastery, after Olympias' goddaughter, Marina.[102]

St Olympias readily gave hospitality, for example, to Bishops Gregory of Nyssa, his brother, Bishop Peter of Sebaste, Onesimus of Pontum and Epiphanius of Cyprus.[103] She knew many bishops of the East: Gregory Nazianzen, Amphilochius of Iconium (whose sister, as noted, was Oympias's mother or governess) and St Basil the Great. Olympias's uncle, Procopius, was a friend of Gregory of Nyssa who dedicated his *Commentary on the Song of Songs* to Olympias.

Although St Olympias had often helped Theophilus of Alexandria he turned against her, undermining her holy reputation because she maintained her affection for his arch-rival, St John Chrysostom.104 Olympias was not only a supporter of Chrysostom, she was his companion, who organised his food,[105] making sure that he was well nourished and that he did not fast to excess as his health was poor, due to excessive asceticism. When Chrysostom was to be banished, Olympias was so devoted to him that *"it was necessary to tear her from his feet by violence"* and she sent him money and medications during his exile.[106] Because she refused to acknowledge the bishop who usurped Chrysostom's position (Arsacius) she, also, was banned from the city.[107] She and Chrysostom's most loyal supporters were accused of burning down a church.

The next bishop in Constantinople (Atticus) exiled or imprisoned Olympias in Nicomedia in 405, with her fifty nuns, although there was no evidence against her.[108] Because she contended for truth the people of Constantinople classed her as 'a confessor'.[109]

Olympia's final years were called *"a lingering martyrdom"* and she was only 41 or 42 at her death in 409/410.[110] Chrysostom had often written to her from his exile to console her. For all his charisma,

Chrysostom spent little time in his see and much in exile, where he died from his privations in 407[111] a few years before Olympias also died. Chrysostom's aunt, Sabaniana,[112] was also, like Olympias, a deaconess.

Having spoken about Basil of Caesarea and Gregory of Nyssa it is time to consider the family from which those brothers came. The story begins with Macrina the Elder whose parents were 'confessors' (having survived the persecutions) and Macrina, herself, and her husband suffered in exile and lost their fortune, because they were Christians.

8.3. St Macrina the Elder (c. 270-340 C.E.)

Macrina, the grandmother of a large family, began as a disciple of the Bishop of Caesarea, St Gregory the Wonderworker (Thaumaturgus) (c.213-c.270), who was himself a disciple of, and an apologist for, Origen of Alexandria.[113] With her husband, who was an advocate and rhetorician, Macrina escaped persecution for three years, surviving in exile in Pontus, suffering hunger, deprivation and loss of property.[114] Afterwards, and when their financial situation improved, they became generous supporters of churches and monasteries. Their son, Basil, married Emmilia (the daughter of a martyr).[115] Nine of their ten children survived: three of whom became bishops (for which St Emmilia is honoured in the Eastern church) and a further two of her children also became saints (St Naucratius and St Macrina the Younger).

8.4. St Emmilia

Upon her widowhood Emmelia moved the family to their property at Annisa in Pontus where St Macrina the Younger established and directed a flourishing ascetic community which lived under her rule and which, for a time, included two of her brothers, Basil and Peter.[116] The monastic Rule of St Basil and his Liturgy, which (much altered) is occasionally used in the East today, may owe much to St Macrina[117] who influenced her siblings and the local community at the family estate in Pontus, for good[118] and encouraged her mother, and others, in the ascetic life.

In total, three of St Emmilia's sons became bishops: St Basil of Caesarea, St Gregory of Nyssa and St Peter of Sebaste. The first two are remembered as 'Cappadocian Fathers'. The illustrious St Basil the Great was closest to his friend, St Gregory, Bishop of Nazianzus, who was the third of the 'Fathers' and who formed part of their group.

8.5. St Macrina the Younger (c.327-379 CE)

Macrina the Younger was the oldest of St Emmilia's ten children.[119] When Macrina the Younger's father, Basil the Elder, died Macrina took over the mothering role, including of their mother, Emmilia, *"whom she led into the ascetic life"*.[120] St Emmelia seems not to have coped well with widowhood nor the tragic death in a fishing accident of her son, the hermit-monk, St Naucratius.

Macrina the Younger became both mother and teacher and her youngest brother, Peter, was entirely home-schooled by her, especially in the Biblical Wisdom literature,[121] so his consecration to the See of Sebaste was a credit to Macrina's Christian learning and knowledge of the Scriptures. Another of Macrina's brothers, Gregory, said of her: "[she was] *Peter's father, teacher, guardian, mother and advisor of every good*".[122] Macrina the Younger's brother, St Gregory, who was known as 'the Theologian' and who became Bishop of Nyssa, seems to have been closer to their sister, Macrina, and was her great admirer. It was this brother, Gregory (c.330-c.395), who wrote Macrina's *Life* (*Vita Macrinae Junioris*) praising her scholarship and her character, and in *On the Soul and the Resurrection* (*De Anima ac Resurrectione*) he praised her competence as a theologian.[123] "*Gregory portrayed Macrina as a woman learned in the Scriptures and capable of reasoned argument and in very exact ways presents her as a Christian Socrates, a Virgin-Teacher, who can expound the truths of the faith out of the experience of her life, and rational knowledge, not only to the other virgins, but even to her brother, the bishop*".[124]

About two years after St Basil's death Gregory visited their sister only to find that she was dying but still well enough to converse with him as she prepared for would have passed silently into history, as so many wonderful, devout and dedicated Christian women have for 2,000 years.

8.6. St Nonna (c.285-374)

St Nonna was raised by Christian parents (Philotatos and Gorgonia) but they had arranged a marriage for her to Gregory, who was a pagan devotee of Hypsistos. They had three children: Gregory, Gorgonia and Caesarius. Nonna devoted years of prayers, fastings and tears before God for her husband's conversion and Gregory the Elder was indeed converted. In a dream he was singing "*I was glad when they said unto me, let us go into the house of the Lord*" (Ps. 122:1). Because

Bishop St Leontius of nearby Caesarea was passing through Nazianzus on his way to the First Ecumenical Council at Nicea (325 CE) Nonna presented her husband to him for baptism. Gregory became a devout and learned Christian and then a bishop and his wife, Nonna, was ordained deaconess at the same time.[125]

Nonna's husband became Bishop Gregory of Nazianzus the Elder, and their older son became Gregory of Nazianzus after him. He was maried to Theosebia. (He was the third of the Cappadocian Fathers noted in the previous section.) St Gorgonia married Alypius and had five children. Their daughters were Alypiani, Eugenia and Nonna and their two sons becane monks. Nonna's nephew was St Amphilochius of Konya/Iconium who was Basil the Great's friend and was the brother of Theodosia, who (as above) was the mother or the governess of St Olympias.[126]

All three of Nonna's children were trained in the Scriptures and Christian devotion. St Caesarius, the physician, died young, in 368, and their daughter, St Gorgonia, in 369/70. She was only 38 years old and left her five children, some still young. Nonna's 100-year-old husband died in 374 and a few months later St Nonna died in church while at prayer.

Philotatos and Gorgonia (Nonna's parents) had at least five grandchildren who became saints: three grandsons (St Gregory and St Caesarius and their cousin St Amphilochius) and two granddaughters (St Gorgonia and her cousin, St Theodosia).

8.7. Were These Women Also Leaders?

These women were remarkable leaders. Their examples and teachings were followed by, not only their own husbands, children and relatives and the many nuns in their monasteries but even of monks, hierarchs and secular rulers.

Chapter 9

Western Women Who Moved East: the Melanias and Paula
9.1. Melania the Elder (c.342-c.410 CE)

Of Melania the Elder's three children only Valerius Publicola survived[127] and he married Albina. Melania's granddaughter was Melania the Younger whose husband was Pinian. Melania's cousin or cousin-in-law was Paulinus of Nola, near Naples (d.431) some of whose correspondence with Melania, Ambrose, Jerome, Augustine and Martin of Tours (316-397) has survived.

Melania the Elder was the aunt of Avita, who was the wife of Apronianus, and the mother of Eunomia.[128] Melania was a spiritual mother to Evagrius of Pontus.[129]

This Melania had no biographer and was largely overlooked because of her role in the 'Origenist controversy' so her *Vita* has to be pieced together from extant letters and a few references. Not only did Rufinus of Aquileia (c.345-c.410) who favoured Origen, live in her double monastery but she, herself, read Origen's works (three million lines of them)[130] and directed her life by them.[131]

Perhaps the taint of Origenism marred her reputation although her theological and biblical knowledge was legendary, as was her knowledge of early Christian texts.

Melania's pagan Spanish parents were Marcellinus, of consular rank, and Caeionia Albina. At the age of fourteen Melania married Valerius Maximus Basilius, Proconsul of Achaea and prefect of Rome from 361 to 363.[132] By the age of twenty-two she had lost her husband and two of her three sons and had moved to Rome where she became a Christian. After ten years Melania left her teenage son, Valerius Publicola, in the care of a guardian and, influenced by St Jerome, she sold property to fund a move with her servants to Egypt[133] where she lived for six months visiting monks and hermits. This is where she met Rufinus of Aquileia, who had been a friend and student companion of Jerome in Rome and who studied Origenism under Didymus the Blind.[134]

Melania is regarded as a 'desert mother' as, when persecution broke out in Egypt after the death of St Athanasius, in 375 A.D., many monks and twelve bishops and priests were banished to Palestine by the Arian emperor, Valens (because they supported the Council of Nicaea).[135]

Melania followed them into exile. The historian Palladius of Helenopolis met some of them who verified the following story: Melania donned slaves' clothing to secretly minister to their needs and was imprisoned for it but her high rank turned her situation around.[136]

Melania's virtue was highly regarded by the Egyptian monks who called her a *female man of God".[137]* Melania must have returned to Egypt as Rufinus of Aquileia, an ex-consul, came there to escort her to Jerusalem where she built monasteries on the Mount of Olives for men and women and distributed food to the local clergy as well as offering hospitality to travellers whom they taught.

Melania the Elder and Rufinus became involved in what is known as the Paulinian schism in Antioch (discussed in 9.4 below) as well as a heresy that challenged the divinity of the Holy Spirit in which they advocated for the Orthodox teaching.[138] Being such champions of orthodoxy it is unfortunate that their regard for Origen has clouded their reputations.

Evagrius of Pontus was Melania's protégée and the source of some information about her. Fellow Spaniard, and a relative, Paulinus of Nola, told his friend, Sulpicius Severus, that Melania had given him a fragment of the true cross, which she had received from Bishop John of Jerusalem (385-417).[139]

When Paulinus of Nola planned to visit the Holy Land with Melania and Rufinus, Jerome discouraged the idea saying, *"it is just as easy to reach the portals of heaven from Britain as from Jerusalem"* (*Ep,* 58.3). Jerome was sour because he was under Bishop John's ban from entering both important churches: the Holy Sepulchre in Jerusalem and the Holy Nativity in Bethlehem.

Jerome's negative attitude and the antagonism between Rufinus and Jerome over Oreginism[140] caused Jerome to change his complementary opinion of Melania. Previously Jerome had called her 'a new Thekla'[141] but later she was *"black in name and black in nature"*.[142]

Melania the Elder lived in Jerusalem, embracing monasticism, carefully shepherding her finances to maintain her own monasteries and devoting herself to good works. Rufinus was also in Jerusalem and they lived together, probably in a double monastery on the Mount of Olives, which she had built.

In 397 Melania and Rufinus returned to Italy where they met with Melania's niece, Anita, and her pagan husband Apronianus, who was instructed in the faith by Melania as she was an excellent teacher and her arguments were persuasive. When he became a Christian, Melania persuaded them and their daughter, Eunomia, to live a life of celibacy.[143]

When Melania began to sell her remaining properties she was opposed by the senators and their wives, whom Palladius called 'wild beasts' but Melania must have had some prophetic insight because she quoted I John 2:18 to them: *"Little children, it is the last hour"*.[144]

In 408, Melania was with a group of refugees (including Melania the Younger, her husband, Pinian, her mother, Albina, and others) who fled to Sicily ahead of the Goths. *"A barbarian hurricane of a kind that had long ago been predicted in prophecy fell on Rome"*.[145] Melania's grandson (Publicola's son) was also taken by her to Sicily where she instructed him in the faith, but this reference is brief and his activities are largely unrecorded.[146] According to Augustine of Hippo, his father, Valerius Publicola had died in Africa in 406.[147] Rufinus died on Sicily in 412 and the others lived in Egypt for seven years on the family estate in Thagaste, near Hippo.

Melania the Elder saved her family and her fortuned and eventually returned to her monastery and died two years later. She must have been a great theologian as she had been deeply involved in the theological debates that were raging in the 4th century, not only about Origen's theories but also about Pelagianism as well as the Paulinist controversy in Antioch. The author of the *The Lausiac History,* Palladius of Helenopolis, was another bishop who was her friend and admirer. He is a source for her life; along with Gerontius[148] and various letters.

9.2. St Paula of Bethlehem (347-404 CE)

Paula's Spanish parents, Blaesilla and Rogatus, were of noble Roman descent[149] and settled in Rome.[150] Although Paula had become a Christian, when she was fifteen years old they arranged a marriage for her to a pagan husband, Toxotius, who was a wealthy senator. Together they had five children (St Blaesilla, Paulina, St Julia Eustochium, Rufina and one son, who was named Toxotius after his father). At the age of 32, Paula was left a wealthy widow. She was grief-stricken but the widow Marcella helped her to find a purpose and hope, greatly influencing her towards the ascetic life.

From c.379, Paula and her family lived in the monastic community that Marcella had established for religious women in her villa in Rome. In 382 Paula met St Jerome, who arrived with St Epiphanius of Salamis (on Cyprus) and Paulinus II of Antioch (the main 'old Nicean' leader, who was central to the Paulinian Controversy discussed in 9.4, below). Jerome then lived with Marcella for three years. Paula arranged marriages for three of her four daughters (Blaesilla, Paula and Rufina). Julia Eustochium, however, was determined to embrace celibacy from the start, although two others did so in widowhood, including St Blaesilla, a young widow who died in 384 because of excessive fasting, under Jerome's direction.

Plate 9.1. Paula, Bethlehem. Photo: D. Campbell, 1988.

When another daughter, Paulina, died in 395 her husband, Pammachius (c.340-410), a senator who was Marcella's cousin and a school-mate of Jerome, became a monkl.[151] Like Marcella, St Pammachius was killed in the Gothic invasion of Rome, in 410 CE. Rufina died in 386.

When Jerome departed from Rome he went to Cyprus to visit Epiphanius of Salamis who was a friend of Paulinian of Tyre (remember that they had visited Rome together) so that Jerome (and Paula) became involved in the Paulinian controversy in Antioch (see 9.4 below).

Of all the holy sites Paula was most moved by those in the Church of the Holy Sepulchre and that of the Holy Nativity, in Bethlehem. Her devotions were extreme. In the former she kissed and licked the holy places and in the latter she entered into the events so fully that she could hear King Herod's little victims crying and in the grotto of the Nativity she prophesised about Bethlehem's importance to redemptive history.[152] Thus, she considered Bethlehem to be the right place to live.[153]

Paula the Elder spent all her money: on cells and monasteries for monks, hostels for pilgrims and three communities for women.[154] She died in debt but Julia Eustochium managed the finances of the monasteries well and reversed their fortunes before she died in 419.

Paula's only daughter-in-law, Laeta, was the mother of little Paula, who was dedicated to virginity at birth, and perhaps of a son, St Eustochius, about whom little is known. It was this Paula, Paula the Younger, who closed St Jerome's eyes in 426, the last of three generations of women who had financed his monastery, cared for him with devotion and assisted his work of translation.

9.3. Jerome or Hieronimus (d. 426 CE).

Jerome, who had had a dissolute youth, arrived in Rome after his conversion and extensive travels in Gaul and Asia, including the two years he spent in Constantinople with John Chrysostom. In Rome he managed to gain entry into aristocratic society (perhaps through his school-friend Pammachius).

Jerome became closely associated with Marcella's group of brown-clad women, so much so that he was accused of sexual impropriety with Paula. After his protector, friend and employer, Pope Damasus, had died Jerome was charged with clerical misconduct by the ecclesiastical court, found guilty and exiled from Rome.[155] Jerome defended himself by publishing copies of letters written by him to both Paula and Marcella, to prove that their contacts had been on a high spiritual plane. These were widely circulated so that at least one side of these relationships is known to posterity.[156]

Paula's daughter, St Blaesilla, had also become a disciple of Jerome before her tragic death from excessive asceticism in 384 and Jerome was blamed, many wanting to stone the monk(s) who had directed her, but Paula supported Jerome.[157] Jerome himself ate so little that, in Bethlehem, his health deteriorated severely until he decided to add olive oil to his meagre, grain-based diet.[158]

Plate 9.2. Jerome, Bethlehem. Photo: D. Campbell, 1988.

When exiled, Jerome planned to live in the Holy Land and persuaded Paula and her daughter, Julia Eustochium, to follow him. In 385 Jerome waited for Paula and Eustochium on the island of Cyprus with Bishop Epiphanius of Salamis. Together Jerome, his brother Paulinian, Paula and Eustochium visited Paulinus II of Antioch in Syria before they all went up to Jerusalem. They stayed with Melania the Elder, whom they had met at Marcella's villa. Jerome's friend Rufinus of Aquilia, who oversaw the monks at Melania's double monastery, was also there. Jerome and his lady companions then toured the Holy Land and visited Egypt, where they stayed with the ascetic monks.

In 386, Jerome wrote, pleading with Marcella to come too, saying *"we adjure you to give back to us the Marcella whom we love"*,[159] but she was already 66 years old and declined, staying in her home until her violent death at the hand of barbarians. Eleven of Jerome's letters to Marcella are extant.[160]

In Rome Marcella had been a mother to them all but in Bethlehem, where Paula and Jerome lived in the separate monasteries which Paula's fortune had founded, Paula took such care of Jerome that she even fed him chicken soup when he was ill. Paula could not be his wife but she was the next best thing: his advisor and motherly companion. He wrote to her and Eustochium every day but the letters are lost except for three letters that he wrote while they were both in Rome. He was devoted to Paula and was with her as she died. They and Eustochium were buried close to each other beneath the Church of the Holy Nativity.

Paula and Eustochium had sailed away leaving Paula's son, Toxotius, a boy of about five, crying for her on the wharf but it was considered a virtue to prove one's devotion by putting Christ first and that was how Jerome presented it.[161] (Similarly, the martyr, Perpetua, when deprived of her nursing-infant before her martyrdom, had seen the renunciation of her child and the rejection of her father's pleas as mere challenges on her path towards God.)[162]

When Paula's son, Toxotius, and his wife, Laeta, had their one daughter, little Paula, Jerome wrote to them in Rome, urging them to permit Paula, the grandmother, to raise and educate the girl in the convent from the age of four. St Julia Eustochium, who took over as abbess when St Paula died, educated the child from the age of seven or eight. Paula the Younger, in her turn, became abbess. St Eustochium was a scholar and a financial manager as, as noted, she paid off her mother's debts and put the monastic community on a sound footing before she died in 419.[163]

Jerome is elevated as a Doctor of the Church and was considered a great theologian and translator of the Greek Bible into Latin (the *Vulgate*)[164] but Paula corrected his errors and edited his work. He had had a troubled youth and was ambitious, manipulative and short tempered. He was emotionally and financially dependent upon his women friends (both Marcella and Paula who were strong and stable characters). Like Origen, Jerome held extreme views of sexual renunciation, arguing that marriage was a necessary evil and *"only for those who cannot attain to the spiritually elite"*.[165] Controversy had raged in Rome when Blaesilla died at age twenty because of excessive fasting, he was criticised and gossiped about because of Paula[166] and he was a centre of numerous doctrinal controversies and argued with St Augustine of Hippo and others about marriage but his views were in keeping with his temperament.

Paula was the grandmother of little Paula and perhaps of a boy, St Eustochius, the children of Toxotius and his wife, Laeta. St Pammachius was her son-in-law (Paulina's widower).[167] In Bethlehem, Paula was an enabler who demonstrated her motherly love for Jerome (and perhaps for his brother and fellow monk, Paulinian) by sublimating her skills and knowledge to Jerome's purposes. Bishop

Palladius recognised this: *"For though she was able to surpass all, having great abilities, He* (Jerome) *hindered her by his jealousy, having induced her to serve his own plan".[168]*

9.4. The Paulinian Controversy (324-381)

Because this disagreement was played out entirely within orthodoxy and was largely confined to Antioch it is kept quiet but it divided the church there for more than half a century. Many of the people discussed in this book were involved: mainly the men, but the women would have been influential behind the scenes.

From the time of St Philogonius, Bishop of Antioch (314-324) a series of bishops held the office briefly before they either died, were ousted or were exiled.

[Paulinus of Tyre (324-25 and then 322), Eulalius (332, two short terms), Ephronius (333-34), Philocius (334), Stephen I (334-41) Leontius (350), Eudoxius (350-54), Aleletus (354), Eudoxius again (354-57), Annanias (357-36) Eudoxius again (360-70) and Dorotheus (370-71) The church was in tumult, ungovernable, because of Arianism, Semi-Arianism and other factionalism. The supporters of the Nicene Creed were divided between 'Old Nicenes' (such as Paulinus of Tyre) and the 'New Nicenes' (such as Meletius who was the newly-elected compromise candidate in 360/361).

Meletius, a gentle-tempered man of sincere piety and pure morals, was trusted and esteemed by John Chrysostom, Gregory of Nazianzus, Gregory of Nyssa and St Basil and he studiously avoided all questions of dispute. After less than a month, however, the Emperor Constantius II (an Arian) banished Meletius on a vague pretext and churches remained in semi-Arian hands, led by one of the former bishops, Paulinus.[169]

When the Emperor died suddenly the new emperor, Julian (361-363), recalled Meletius from Armenia but, before his arrival, Paulinus of Tyre was consecrated Bishop of Antioch in 371.[170] That meant that there were three claimants to the see: the Eustathians (led by Paulinus, the 'official bishop from 371 to 376), the Arians, who had separate churches (led by Bishop Evagrius) and the New Niceans, who were led by Meletius. Emperor Julian (who was called 'the Apostate') harassed and tormented all Christians, orthodox or Arian, but he was killed in battle and the mild mannered Jovian reigned.

Jovian ordered St Athanasius of Alexandria, to come to Antioch. Because Meletius did not respond to the Patriarch's offer of communion Athanasius entered into communion with Paulinus of Tyre. The Arians then triumphed under a new emperor, Valens (364-378), who persecuted orthodoxy and exiled Meletius to Armenia from 365 to c.367. Persecution against Orthodoxy restarted in 371 and Meletius was again banished.[171]

St Basil, St Jerome and Pope Damasus then entered the fray, along with another orthodox group who claimed loyalty to St Athanasius. The Pope, who didn't really understand the issues, recognised Paulinus as bishop and made him the papal legate (representative) in the East. Basil and then Jerome intervened by direct appeals to the Pope, to whom Basil also sent two ambassadors. The Pope responded by condemning Arianism (in 379). Meanwhile Jerome, who had arrived in Antioch, although he did not consider himself an Arian, did associate himself with Paulinus (whom he met in Marcella's house in Rome) and Jerome must have accepted his authority because he consented to being ordained a priest by Paulinus, provided he could continue to live as a monk.[172]

The new emperor, Gratian, recalled Meletius but Paulinus refused all offers of compromise. The next emperor, Theodosius I, deposed the Arian bishop of Constantinople, Demosphilus, and appointed Gregory Nazianzus as Patriarch before calling a Council to ratify the decision. In 380, Gregory Nazianzus (who later resigned) was enthroned by Meletius in the Great Church (although the Church now recognises Vitalius not Meletius as having been bishop at that time).[173] Pope Damasus convened a Council in Rome to discuss the schism in Antioch and the next year Meletius died in Constantinople, leaving the field of battle.[174] His funeral was attended by the pious emperor, Theodosius I. In 376 Paulinius had been replaced by Vitalius who was the bishop for eight years. Paulinus died in 388.

Churchmen from Egypt, Palestine, Rome and Constantinople were involved in this quarrel, which illustrates the turmoil that often operated during the entire 4th century church and the passions with which male hierarchs fought for their status and their opinions. (By comparison, the leading women of the period were voices of reason.) It did great damage to the church. The controversy was partly theological and partly a clash of personalities. It was important because Antioch was an ancient see and its second bishop had been St Peter (c.45-53 A.D.) although it did not become a Patriarchate until after the Council of Chalcedon, in 451.

The Emperor Theodosius I, who was staunchly Orthodox, went on to pass anti-Arian laws. He was a wise ruler whose long reign helped to establish orthodoxy.[175] In 380 he decreed that Christianity (those in communion with Damasus of Rome and Peter of Alexandria) was the official religion of the Empire.[176] After Theodosius I died his territory was divided between his sons. Arcadius ruled the East and Honorius the West, and the Pope (who was the only Patriarch in the West) would go on to be more prominent.

9.5. The Origenist Controversy (393-397 and 398-401 C.E.)

No sooner had the dust settled after the Paulinist controversy in Antioch and the East than the church was rocked by another major theological dispute, regarding Origen. The teachings of Origen, the famed philosopher-theologian and a Doctor of the Church, came into question long after his death. He had been tortured in the Decian persecution and had died in 254, aged 69.[177]

Previously, the young Origen had been so successful in Alexandra and abroad, in both Christian and pagan philosophy, that his bishop had become suspicious and, in 231, Origen had been defrocked and banished to the Holy Land. There, the bishops of Jerusalem and Caesarea had welcomed him[178] and he set up his school at Caesarea where St Pamphilus the Martyr had established a library which probably helped Origen to write his best works: his *Commentary on St John* and his *Commentary on Song of Songs*. This was the same library which the church historian Eusebius (c.260-340) would utilised. Eusebius wrote an *Apology for Origen*, which was suspect because Eusebius, himself, was already considered to be semi-Arian.

The two main Origenist doctrines that caused most controversy were: the "pre-existence of the soul" *and the* "restoration of all things" *(Universalism)*. These were seen as minimising or denying the Incarnation and disparaging the body in favour of the spirit (in the Greek manner). Late in the 4th century doubts were expressed by Bishop Epiphanius of Salamis about Origen's orthodoxy which triggered the controversy over his divergent beliefs, especially his Universalism.

In 393, Epiphanius of Salamis, who was formerly a monk in Palestine, was invited by Bishop John of Jerusalem to preach a sermon in the Church of the Anastasis/Resurrection. He denounced Origenism but was offended because Bishop John did not support him. In 394 Bishop Epiphanius ordained Jerome's brother, the monk Paulinian, in Bethlehem, and Bishop John was angry that his canonical jurisdiction had been violated. The two patched things up by letter and in so doing Epiphanius provided seven doctrinal issues by which Origenism was corrupting monks in the East, including the teaching that *"the devil will return to his former dignity and rise again to the kingdom of heaven"*.[179]

Naturally the bishops mentioned in this chapter were in the thick of the controversy, as was Melania the Elder because of her own association with Oreginism and her very close association with Rufinus of Aquileia, who lived in the monastery she had built on the Mount of Olives. Back in Rome, Marcella became involved because of her vigorous pursuit of orthodoxy. Jerome, who had previously praised Melania the Elder, turned against her; although he, Paula and Melania the Elder had all been taught by Marcella and they must once have been good friends.

These two ordained monks, Jerome and Rufinus, who were indeed old friends, having met in a monastery in Aqueleia, became embroiled in controversy because each had translated Origen's work and both were therefore thought by others to condone his views. Each tried to establish that the other was the more Origenist, and therefore more of a heretic. They bitterly opposed each other's opinion. The translation of the Bible into Latin (the *Vulgate*) was Jerome's greatest achievement but Rufinus attacked his right to use the Jews' Hebrew text to translate the Septuagint or LXX (the Old Testament in Greek) into Latin: and to have a heretic (a Jew) help him do it!! He behaved as if he thought that the Greek LXX was the God-given original, rather than having been, itself, a Greek translation made by Jews from previously known Hebrew texts, which were all written by Jews.

The upshot of the conflict was that Bishop John of Jerusalem appealed to the Pope, and Theophilus of Alexandria mediated peace. John, Jerome and Rufinus were reconciled in 397[180] but a year later Rufinus (unwisely) translated Eusebius' *Defense of Origen* and two works by Origen himself and stated that Jerome had smoothed over difficult parts of Origen to make them acceptable to Latin readers. Now Jerome was branded as dishonest as well as an Origenist.

Jerome responded by producing a new translation in which he pointed to where Rufinus had softened Origen's text. The two corresponded. Jerome wrote a conciliatory letter but it was never delivered. Jerome's moderate position was rather uncharacteristic of him but matters were taken over by Theophilus of Alexandria (no longer a peace-maker) who successfully petitioned Pope Anastasius I to ban the use of Origen's writings in monasteries, because of the damage being done by them in Egypt.

Theophilus of Alexandria was heavy handed against the Egyptian monasteries and was called to Constantinople, by Emperor Arcadius and the Patriarch, John Chrysostom, to apologise. Theophilus then sought revenge against Chrysostom and successfully colluded with the Empress Eudoxia to have the Patriarch exiled. They had been rivals for the see of Constantinople and Theophilus had lost out so it wasn't hard for him to oppose Chrysostom on other issues.

Meanwhile, in Rome, Marcella and Jerome's friend (who was Paula's son-in-law) St Pammachius (c.340-410),[181] were gathering witnesses to testify against the heresies of Origen before Pope Anastasius I.[182] Rufinus wrote in a deferential tone to the Pope saying that he was merely a translator and declaring his orthodoxy and his appreciation of Papal authority. The Pope condemned Origenism but handed Rufinus's case back to his bishop, John of Jerusalem. At the same time that Marcella was leading an anti-Origenist campaign her friend, Melania the Elder, was still allied with Rufinus, who, despite his protestations, was not entirely free of doctrinal suspicion.

Both Jerome and Theophilos of Alexandria had both supported Origenism but changed their opinions and became opponents. Jerome's past beliefs continued to be used against him as the war of words against Originism heated up. A century later, during Emperor Justinian's reign (527-565) Origenism was finally declared heretical by the Second Council of Constantinople in 553.[183]

9.6. A Note About Pelagianism

The British monk Pelagius taught against the idea of original sin and held that human choice comes before divine grace in the conversion process, that the person was solely responsible for their own moral choices, that the Law and the Gospel permit entrance to heaven and that all do not die because of Adam, nor will all rise because of Christ's resurrection.[184] This view was contrary to the teachings of St Augustine of Hippo, who was virtually a predestinarian and a strong opponent of Pelagianism.

Pelagius had success from 400 C.E. in Rome where he met the British lawyer, Celestius/Coelestius. After the sack of Rome in 410 they went together to Carthage where Augustine and other African bishops opposed them. Celestius then went to Ephesus and Pelagius went to Palestine where he was supported by the infamous Nestorius.[185] Pelagius was attacked by Augustine, Jerome and Paulinus of Milan before being opposed or excommunicated by two Popes and eventually condemned by two Synods and five Councils. Imperial edicts were issued against both Pelagius and Celestius after the Council of Carthage (417) although eighteen bishops were deposed for being reluctant or unwilling to subscribe.[186] Pelagianism continued in Southern Gaul and parts of Britain but disappeared in the 6th century.[187]

9.7. Melania the Younger

As noted, Melania the Younger's parents were Publicola and Albina. At fourteen she married Valerius Pinianus (Pinian) who was seventeen. Seven years into their marriage Pinian reluctantly agreed that they would live celibate, dedicated lives together as she had almost died in childbirth and neither of her babies had survived.[188] Melania had said, *"if God had wished us to have children, He would not have taken away my children untimely"*.[189]

Pinian and Melania were each extremely wealthy but, despite great opposition, they quickly sold assets and properties to fund monasteries. As previously noted, in c.408, they fled from Rome to Egypt, via Sicily, with others and, although Rufinus of Aquileia died in Sicily, the others reached Africa.[190]

Plate 9.3. St Melania the Younger (c.383/5–c.439 C.E.)

Historian Peter Brown notes a culture-clash between the many Roman wealthy, aristocratic Christian refugees from Alaric's invasion of Rome and the provincial Christianity of Africa.[191] This is illustrated in Melania's and Pinian's lives in that the local congregation of Thagaste, where they owned property, clamoured for St Augustine of Hippo to ordain Pinian so that he (and his wealth) would remain there. His wife, Melania, or her grandmother, intervened and refused, so instead they founded two monasteries at Thagaste, promised that if Pinian was ever to seek ordination it would be at Hippo and departed; *"leaving Augustine to sort out the mess".[192]*

In 417 they journeyed to Bethlehem to join St Jerome. In Palestine in 418 they met with the English monk, Pelagius, and Melania wrote to Augustine in positive terms about his views but Augustine did not approve, and said so.[193] Pinian died in 431 and Melania founded another monastery on the Mount of Olives, although she chose not to be the Mother Superior.[194] Melania continued her generosity to monks, churches and the poor. Gerontius regarded her as *a divinely inspired teacher*: *"Her whole concern was to teach the sisters in every way about spiritual works and virtues, so that they could present the virginity of their souls and the spotlessness of their bodies to their heavenly Bride-groom and Master Christ".*[195]

Gerontius also recounted three miracles for suffering women that Melania the Younger facilitated, of the many he could have described.[196] In 437, Melania travelled to Constantinople to visit her pagan uncle and experienced his death-bed conversion. She prayed for the Empress Aelia Eudocia's injured ankle to be healed. Upon Melania's return to Jerusalem, the empress visited the Holy Land and Melania led her on an extended pilgrimage to the biblical sites. They were very close friends. Her biographer said they *"were scarcely able to be separated from one another, for they were strongly bonded together in spiritual love".*[197] Very soon after the Empress Eudocia returned to Constantinople, when Melania the Younger was 55 years old and had been living in her own monastery for about twenty years, she died, in 439.[198]

Much can be learned about ascetic women from Melania's extensive *Vita* including that they enjoyed the freedom to travel as widely as they themselves chose. For example, after she and Pinian vowed celibacy it was Melania who took the leadership and decided where they would live.[199]

9.8. Conclusions

Although the Christian women of the 4th to 5th centuries are largely forgotten or sidelined they were deeply involved and very influential in all of the big issues within the church and between churchmen. It was not a case of 'women should be seen and not heard'. These ladies were educated and intelligent and promoted their opinions. Being abbesses of their own monasteries and/or widows with independent means they were able to travel and to reside where they chose and do what work they chose to do. By comparison married women were subservient, obedient to their husbands, cumbered with domestic responsibilities, confined to home, excluded from having friendships with other men and restricted by conventional expectations. Add to this the burden of an arranged marriage: having intimate relations with a man they might not even like, and the bearing (and burying) of numerous children.

If celibacy could be embraced it was an ideal, interesting and fulfilling life with the added bonuses of God's favour in this life and rewards in Eternity. Even though women had already been excluded from sacramental roles and a strict hierarchy had developed these ladies crossed class and social barriers and gave objective advice, even to popes and empresses. They followed their own spiritual paths and claimed sovereignty over themselves.

Chapter 10
Women of the Syrian Church
10.1. Documents Compiled by the Syrian Church

There are a number of surviving documents that were utilised in the Eastern Church and which concern praxis, church governance and women. They are:

The *Didascalia Apostolorum* (early-3rd century)

The *Apostolic Constitutions* (4th century)

The *Testamentum Domini* (4th-5th century)

10.2. Women's Leadership: In Syria

Two Syrian documents were very closely related in that the earlier one, the early-3rd-century *Didaskalia Apostolorum*, was incorporated into the later, the 4th-century *Apostolic Constitutions*. Together they provide information about what Christian women were permitted to do in Asia.

The *Didascalia Apostolorum* 2.26; 3.12 stated that a bishop must appoint a woman for the ministry of women:

"we say that the ministry of a woman deacon is especially needed and important, For our Lord and Savior was ministered to by women ministers, 'Mary Magdalene, and Mary the daughter of James and mother of Jose, and the mother of the sons of Zebedee' (Matt. 27:56) and other women besides. And you also need the ministry of a deaoness for many things".[200]

According to the *Didascalia Apostolorum* [201] female deacons (or deaconesses) could not teach at this time, but instructed women catechumens, gave pastoral ministry and may have baptised women, a 2nd-3rd-century usage that Tertullian railed against[202] - so much so that it must have occurred.[203]

Considering that the candidates were baptised while naked, today that would be considered more seemly, irrespective of clerical territorialism and claims. The female deaconate did not cease, however, as in the 4th century there was a rite for the ordination of female deacons with the laying on of hands and prayer for the Holy Spirit.[204] Female deacons were considered essential and at least 61 examples have been found in the East.[205]

The slightly later document (of the 4th-5th-century) the *Testamentum Domini*, which survived only in Syriac, noted that women of the Order of Widows sat with the bishop and clergy and were given precedence over women deacons.[206] The *Testamentum Domini* also mentions women presbyters[207] (which funerary inscriptions also support)[208] but this was not an official document of the Trinitarian/Catholic Church and may have been compiled by Syrian Monophysites.[209]

Both the *Didaskalia* and the *Apostolic Constitutions*, being Syrian documents, provide information about what Christian women were permitted to do in Asia. Only widows and virgins had any formal role but they would not have been idle because there were many females in the church; for numerous reasons. More pagan wives converted than husbands (notably men of senatorial rank feared losing their status by converting) and the exposure of unwanted babies (usually girls) was forbidden to Christians (and Jews) although common in the Roman Empire.[210] After 300, when monasticism became popular, more men entered remote desert monasteries than women entered convents. It was Cyprian of Carthage (North Africa) in his *Testimonia* (c.255) who noted the number of maidens for whom it was difficult to find husbands.[211]

10.3. What Did Deaconesses Do?

(1) Female deacons/deaconesses visited women at home, even going into pagan homes to bathe the sick. They entered women's space (e.g., rooms and courtyards) to view parts of the female body that men were not to see (for example to give assistance or medical advice).

(2) They entered the baptismal waters to complete the anointing of women converts after the bishop had annointed the head. They received women (presumably from the water).

(3) They taught and instructed women converts about purity and holiness, both before and after their baptism.

(4) They stood at the women's entrances to churches to indicate spare seats and kept the women and children in order.[212]

(5) One important service (which should have been maintained) was that of chaperoning women who had dealings with bishops and other clergy.[213]

(6) They delivered messages and served wherever needed:

"Let both the Deacons and the Deaconesses be ready to carry messages, to travel about, to minister and serve" (*Apost. Constitutions* II, 57,58).

In the East, women had participated in formal ministry in the 1st to early 2nd century although the order of deaconess declined as adult baptisms declined. An extant rite of Episcopal ordination for deaconesses dates from the 8th century.

The Order was never abolished and today there are examples of deaconesses in Greek and Armenian convents.[214]

10.4. Requirements and Ordination

According to Canon 15 of the Council of Chalcedon on 451 A.D. deaconesses must be over 40 years old and must not marry after ordination.[215]

"Ordain also a deaconess, faithful and holy for the service to women" (*Apostolic Constitutions 3.16.1*).

Concerning the ordination of a deaconess, in the presence of presbyters, deacons and deaconesses, with the laying on of hands the bishop will say:

"O eternal God, the Father of our Lord Jesus Christ, the creator of man and woman, who filled with the Spirit Miriam, Deborah, Anna and

Huldah...[216] who did not judge it unworthy that your only-begotten Son should be born of a woman, who also in the tent of witness and in the temple appointed women as guardians of your holy gates; look now upon this woman, your servant, who has been chosen for the diaconate, and give her the Holy Spirit, and 'purify her from every defilement of the flesh and spirit [II Cor. 7:1] so that she may worthily accomplish the work with which she has been entrusted, for your glory and the praise of your Christ, through whom be glory and adoration in you in the Holy Spirit forever. Amen".[217]

Chapter 11
The Augusta Aelia Eudocia: Empress and Patron

Athenaís was the beautiful daughter of Leontis, a pagan teacher of rhetoric at the famous Academy of Athens:[218] although his origins were, perhaps, in Antioch.[219] Leontis trained his daughter in rhetoric, philosophy, and literature, especially Homer's poetry. When he died, Athenaís was taken by female relatives to Constantinople to contest her father's will which had left her only 100 gold coins while her two younger brothers inherited very substantial wealth.

In the capital Athenaís received instruction in Christianity and was baptised by the Partriarch Atticus, taking the name Eudocia.[220] There are legends about how she came to be married to the twenty-year old Emperor Theodosius II (c.401-460) but she did marry him, in 421 A.D. After the birth of her first child, Lucinia Eudoxia, in 422, she was granted the title, Augusta Aelia Eudocia, by which she outranked the Emperor's domineering sister, Pulcharia, who was a powerful rival to the empress but who no longer lived in the palace, but had her own court.[221] Lucinia Eudoxia, was their only child to survive and, at the age of fifteen (in 437) she was married to her cousin, the Western Emperor Valentinian III, (425-455). With his mother (Galla Placidia) and his sister (Honoria), he had taken refuge in Constantinople as he had been replaced by a usurper, John. It took an army from the East to defeat John and restore Valentinian III, as was visibly demonstrated when his regalia (his diadem and *paludamentum*) were transported from the East and conferred upon him in 425.[222]

Back in 417, Melania the Younger, her husband, Pinian, and her grandmother had left North Africa to travel to Bethlehem to join St Jerome and there they met the English monk, Pelagius. One might imagine the learned and intense theological discussions which ensued and in which Melania the Younger engaged so intensely that she wrote to Augustine of Hippo in positive terms about Pelagius's views (although Augustine did not approve, and said so).[223]

Soon they would go to the long-established monastery on the Mount of Olives, founded by Melania the Elder. Pinian died in 431 and Melania founded another monastery on the Mount of Olives, while continuing her generosity to monks, churches and the poor.

As noted above in Chapter 9, in 437 Melania the Younger travelled to Constantinople to visit her pagan uncle and experienced his death-bed conversion. She prayed for the Empress Aelia Eudocia's injured ankle to be healed and, on the basis of this relationship, and because Eudocia's daughter, Lucinia Eudoxia, was by now married, the Empress decided to spend a year on pilgrimage, with Melania guiding her around the sacred sites of the Holy Land (in 438 A.D.).[224] It is said that Melania had begged and pleaded with the Emperor to permit his wife to make the pilgrimage, but it is uncertain whether Melania, for all her wealth, had such influence.

In the course of her journey to Jerusalem Eudocia visited Antioch: apparently it was a state visit as the Empress was welcomed and feted. She donated money for the repair of buildings and eloquently addressed the Senate.

As a result one gold and one bronze statue of her were erected in the city.[225]

Empress Eudocia returned from Jerusalem to Constantinople with relics of St Stephen and/or St Peter's chains. Half of the chains were sent to her daughter, Lucinia Eudoxia, in the West and the Pope built a basilica to house them: St Peter ad Vincula.[226]

In 441, Eudocia fell into disgrace and perhaps was banished from court under a cloud of suspicion of adultery with the Emperor's close friend Paulinus.

Perhaps, however, her sister-in-law, the Augusta Pulcharia, was too powerful a rival and there was no longer enough room for them both at court. Whatever is the true background story the emperor *"did not withdraw her imperial distinction"*[227] nor her access to money.

Plate 11.1. Gold coin the Augusta Aelia Eudocia. Copyright: Trustees of the British Museum.

Having built the Church of St Polyeuctos in Constantinople, the Augusta Eudocia had developed an interest in church-biuilding and leaving permanent donations in sacred places. In Jerusalem, her major building projects included strengthening the city walls and building an Episcopal palace and more great churches, including St Stephen's just outside the city, where she was buried.

On the Empress Eudocia's gold coins (Plate 11.1) she is depicted wearing a *loros* and a diadem (tiara) (which is still exclusive to royal women) and she is crowned by the hand of God: a claim to divine appointment. She is identified as a saint on a full-lenth, but stylised, image of her dressed in her attire as a Byzantine empress in coloured stone which is now in the Istanbul Museum.

Although her husband was still alive, Eudocia returned to live permanently in Jerusalem in 443 A.D. (although her friend and guide, Melania, had died). She left the power struggle to Pulcharia who, although dedicated to virginity, 'married' Marcian and elevated him to the throne when her brother died without a male heir.

For a period of her time in Jerusalem Eudocia was a Monophysite (as was common in the East) but she was reconciled to Orthodoxy and was readmitted, becaming an ardent supporter of the Council of Chalecdon. The Christology of this Council was adopted by the Eastern bishops at first, but later repudiated in favour of Monophysitism. Adhering to Chalcedon was the difference between being orthodox and unorthodox, basically the difference between the West and the majority of the East.

In her later years Eudocia devoted herseld to religious writing. She completed a substantial body of literature, only a little of which has survived. It included poetry (including a poem inscribed in Galilee, in the warm baths at Hamat Gader/Gadera), a life of Saints Cyprian and Justina of Antioch in three books and her Homeric cento (2,344 lines of an epic poem incorporating Homer and Scriptural references).[228]

During her year-long pilgrimage with Melania the Younger the Empress Eudocia would have met all of the ascetics and theologically important people who were still alive and residing in the many monasteries dotted throughout the country. She saw a great many sites, including Hamat Gader/Gadera, a Roman-era bath which is situated near where water from the Lake of Galilee runs into the Jordan River, on its way to the Dead Sea, and which utilised natural hot springs.

Eudocia's charitable works, buildings and donations in the Holy Land were exemplary, executed in the same spirit as those of a former Empress, the Augusta Helena, the mother of Constantine I, by whose efforts the Church of the Holy Sepulchre and the Church of the Holy Nativity had been built a century earlier. Eudocia's husband, the Emperor Theodosius II, did not curtail her acces to money and she owned a vast personal fortune including lands in Palestine.[229] She retained her imperial distinction, the title Augusta, which meant that her *basiléia* remained: she was still the Empress, conducting affairs from her palace in Bethlehem.

Chapter 12

Cerula, Bitalia, Cominia and Ilaritas

12.1. Introduction

There are many holy women buried in Christian catacombs in Rome, Naples and elsewhere whose names are known but whose biographies remain mysteries. We can only guess at their stories by their inscriptions and how they are presented. The orants (or orantes) pose, with raised hands, indicates their holiness as it is known as the pose of prayer. Some scholars think that it indicates clerical status[230] but the child, Nonnosa, the daughter of Theotecnus and Ilaritas depicted between them in the Catacomb of St Gennaro in Naples (Plate 12.1) was only two years old. She would not have been ordained as this was never just an honorary status that could be conferred upon children.

Plate 12.1. Theotecnus and Ilaritas with Nonnosa, Catacomb of St Gennaro, Naples.[231]

Women did receive ordination but that fact must be deduced by other means, not by the orants pose. One means is by funerary inscriptions, an issue that has been thoroughly analysed by Kevin Madigan and Caroline Osiek[232] who have identified inscriptions of one female bishop and five women called *presbytera* (or similar) from the West and for four women presbyters (priests) in the East as well as sixty-one female deacons there.[233]

12.2. Cerula and Bitalia

Clothing and attributes were intentionally included and conveyed deliberate messages. The similar images of Cerula and Bitalia in the Catacomb of St Gennaro are both are dated late 5th to early 6th century. Note the Christogram, the Constantinian monogrphy Chi-Rho: this is the sign which Constantine saw in the sky and which prompted him to favour Christianity, win the Empire in battle and end the persecutions. Its use was well established soon after Constantine became sole ruler and it is painted above the heads of both Cerula and Bitalia (Plates 12.2 and 12.3).

Plate 12.2. Deceased woman Cerula, Catacomb of St Gennaro, Naples.[234]

In Cerula's case the Greek letters Alpha and Omega are visible. They allude to Jesus Christ as the beginning and the end (according to the Greek alphabet) and a reference from Revelation 22:13.

The images of Cerula and Bitalia are similarly presented although Bitalia's is in a more degraded state (air-brushed in Plate 12.3 for clarity). While women were portrayed in Pompeii with a pencil and codex (book) to denote literacy and on Roman sarcophagi with an unfurled or rolled scroll, these two women are depicted here with the four open gospels that are lapped by tongues of fire. This is a unique iconography and must have held important meaning. Fortunately, in Cerula's case the inscriptions are still visible: Mark and John at her right hand and Luke and Matthew at her left. Other than Cerula's name, the only other inscription is "*in Peace*". There is just enough of the word 'Matthew' at Bitalia's left hand to know that the gospels are indicated there also, but in a different order. The Holy Word of the four gospels is alive for (or within) these two women.These attributes apply in both cases and they indicate that Cerula and Bitalia were not just literate but learned in the Scriptures: devoted Christian of considerable importance buried as wealthy women, in graves with their own arcisolia and painted portrait. In Cerula's case an image of St Paul is still visible on her right. Perhaps St Peter was originally on her left. The open gospels, aflame, raise the possibility that our two learned women served in teaching the Word, as well as strudying it.

Now to consider Cerula's clothing. As I have argued in my doctoral thesis, poor women were characteristically depicted wearing one layer of clothing, even torn clothing, whereas wealthy and aristocratic women were depicted with three (or more) layers.[235] Cerulia wears three garments: a white robe, a caftan or dalmatic over that and a short overlay, like a pallium or a poncho, well camouflaging the breast area. A similar but longer garment is worn by three or more women courtiers in the 'Empress Theodora' panel at San Vitale, Ravenna (of the 6th century). This garment is read as suggesting priesthood but a close inspection of Cerula's over-garment shows that it is patterned with rows of dancing figures, each adopting a different pose. Although they may be clothed (which dancing girls often were not, in ancient depictions)[236] they were a common Egyptian motif, with origins in Egyptian paganism, and are most unlikely to have graced the vestments of an Italian cleric of the 5th-6th century, male or female.

Plate 12.3. Deceased woman Bitalia, Catacomb of St Gennaro, Naples. Public domain.

The only indication of jewellery seen on Cerula and Bitalia are two wide wrist-bracelets which are either of yellow enamel or gold. Either way, they would have indicated that the woman was affluent, as bracelets of metals such as iron, bronze or silver-alloy were worn by poor women.[237] Although these women's hairstyles are carefully indicated there is no suggestion of rouge or lipstick, nor the necklaces and drop ear-rings with multiple pendoulia characteristic of funerary portraits of wealthy women in Antiquity. Both Bitalia and Cerula are veiled. All of this indicates that they followed the principles of women's attire taught by Tertullian (c.190-220 A.D.) who greatly influenced the Latin Church, including in Italy, because he wrote in Latin. Tertulian had condemned women who wore mascara and rouge and used face creams to lighten their skin and who wore gold and silver jewellery, precious stones, and pearls. He also railed against professed virgins who took advantage of their right, as single women, not to wear a veil in church and against women who taught and baptised when they should *"keep silence"* as St Paul said (I Cor. 14:34).[238]

All of this satisfactorily accounts for the way Cerula and Bitalia are depicted without recourse to a claim that they were prtiests or church officials but for the fact that, at exactly that time (the late 5th century) the Pope, Gelasius I, was critical of bishops who permitted women in Southern Italy to serve at sacred altars and undertake all tasks usually entrusted to men... which he said was *"not appropriate"*.[239] There is no close link between these burials and the Pope's letter but a link is possible.

A comparison will be made between the attire of these two and the similar attire worn by the two other women who are buried nearby: Cominia (in Plate 10.4) and Ilaritas in Plate 10.1.

Interestingly, while Ilaritas only wears bracelets her child is laden with jewellery: huge earrings, a coronet, a broach, bracelets and a necklace that resembles a double row of pearls. It seems that women had to be unadorned while girls could display the family jewells. Furthermore a crown is depicted hovering above the child's head, an attribute that usually suggested martyrdom, but cannot be accounted for.

10.4. Cominia and her daughter, Nicatiola.

The woman, Cominia, who is buried with her daughter, Nicatiola, is presented as an undecorated, unadorned holy woman: an orant, veiled and completely in white. Perhaps she too was a woman of importance with a high function in the church as theirs is the oldest burtial in the Catacomb of Saint Gennaro and the saint is depicted with them in the arcosolium.

Perhaps this burial was the purpose for which this particular catacomb was created, although other (pagan) burials in Naples were centuries older.

Particular attention has been paid to clothing because clothing was very important to women of the period. It announced their status and gave them a public identity.[241] There were appropriate outfits to define widows, prostitutes, matrons, rich women, imperial women, poor women and the unmarried. Veils, which so exercised the minds of churchmen such as Tertullian, were just one example.

Plate 12.4. St Gennaro between Nicatiola and her mother, Cominia. Catacomb St Gennaro, Naples.[240]

10.5. Conclusions

The data available indicates the piety and wealth of the four named women: Cerula and Bitulia, and the mothers Cominia and Ilaritas buried in these catacombs in Naples. But just as the attributes of the two year old child, Nonnsa, probably did not represent reality but were merely indicating favour, wealth and bounty so the clothing and attributes of the women. They may not have been aristocrats, simply presented as such as a compliment to their status in the Christian community but the manner of their burials suggests affluence if not weath.

Were they leaders? Every mother is a leadrer at least to her children and two of the women had at least one child (and perhaps other surviving children). Funerary images and inscriptions went on consoling or instructing the viewing public long after the burial. The image of Saint Gennaro would have drawn viewers to this catacomb, while the images of Cerula and Bitalia would have taught a message: the gospels are important; they are holy fire.

As for epigraphic evidence to support an interpretation that any of these four women could have been ordained clerics, Madigan and Osiek have found very few such inscriptions in Italy: one *eposcopa* in Rome, one *presbytera* in each of Brittium and Sicily and an inscription for one female deacon in Rome; and none at all in Naples (although inscriptions for sixty-one female deacons were found in the East).[242] The argument against their holding sacramental office must not detract from the rich evidence that they were important, enlightened, holy women.

Attributes such as the orants pose, the pairs of lighted candles, the family members also depicted as orants, the Christogram (Chi-Roh), the A and ω, the hovering crown and their garments and veiled heads are designed to inform the viewer of the virtues and qualities of these deceased women (including as wives and mothers or as women fervently devoted to the Scriptures) and to set them in an appropriate holy setting. The open, flaming gospels, being unique, are the most important icons.

Chapter 13

Conclusions

13.1. Mary and Priscilla: Women of the Post-Apostolic Period

As the archaeology of Ephesus is still revealing, it was a great city, growing in size and glory and enhanced by the pagan emperors Claudius, Domition and Trajan with temples, baths and theatres. St Paul ministered there and wrote to its church. His friends, Prisca and Aquila, settled there and assumed leadership roles. The survival on Paul's epistle demonstrated its value to the Ephesian church.

Of course neither St Paul nor Luke-Acts make mention of it as it happened after Paul's martyrdom, but there are strong traditions that St John lived and died there,[243] that the Virgin Mary settled there and that Mary Magdalene came there after evangelising in Rome and lived with the Virgin Mary before being buried there.[244] Eusebius states that St Philip and some of his four daughters who had prophetic gifts,[245] were buried in nearby Hieropolis and one daughter was buried in Ephesus.[246] One must remember that, if St John lived to a great age, his knowledge of the words of Jesus endured in Ephesus for three decades after Paul's epistles were written. Ephesus was the centre of Eastern Christianity for a time.

The magnificent Library of Ephesus was commenced in c.114 and completed in c.125 A.D. but the Goths destroyed the city, including the Temple of Artemis, in 262/265 A.D., although Constantine tried to restore it in the 4th century.

After 70 A.D. Jerusalem lay in ruins, although the Judaeo-Christians under the leadership of St James and then Symeon-ben-Clopas had returned from their self-imposed exile in the East after 70 C.E. and probably lived around the slopes of Mt Zion. The historian Eusebius advises us that a vast number of the circumcision believed in Christ and that the Jerusalem church was then led by a succession of Judaeo-Christians, and that a bishop Justus came after Symeon.[247] The once-prominent women leaders of the 1st century are no longer mentioned.

Plate 13.1. Celsus Library, Ephesus, Photograph: D. Campbell, 1995.

13.2. Innovations of the Post-Apostolic Period

As the above discussion of St Thekla's narrative explains, from the 2nd century celibacy had been promoted as the only way to guarantee one's own salvation so that those who wanted to truly follow Christ had to embrace that pathway and the men they obviously loved had to do the same. In the case of Melania the Younger and her husband Pinian they embraced celibacy within marriage because Melania had lost two children and had almost died herself, but in other cases it was a choice prompted by devotion and religious belief.

All sorts of psychological and sociological reasons are put forward to explain the rush into monasteries but the great influence of two early 2nd century apocryphal documents is the simplest explanation and one cannot over-estimate their influence: the *Protevangelium or Book of James and the Acts of Paul and Thekla*. Although *The Acts of Thekla* (within the latter) is little known in the West the art and artefacts left behind after the centuries demonstrate the influence of these apocryphal documents: eulogia of Thekla, girls named Thekla, images of the (extra-biblical) trial of the Virgin by bitter waters and of the Virgin spinning a purple curtain in the Temple and of the midwives at her delivery are all derived from one or other of these two sources.

The *Protevangelium of James* established a proof that the Virgin Mary remained a virgin even after giving birth. As this was clearly a miracle, God must have been demonstrating that virginity was exemplary, even necessary for holiness (otherwise why make such a point of it). The *Acts of Thekla* taught that one can only be certain of Heaven's bliss if one is a life-long celibate and God apparently confirmed that by miraculously delivering Thekla during numerous attempts to martyr her (one can contrast this with the martyrdoms of Perpetua and Felicitas, both young mothers, who were not rescued).

The *Acts of Thekla* and the *Book of James* [248] told Christians what everyone wanted or needed to know... extra information that the gospels don't tell us about the details (even the intimate details) of Mary the Mother and St Paul. The reception of these two works trumped that of the New Testament so their teachings prevailed in the post-apostolic period.

Unfortunately for the future of the church the leading men, who embraced at least the idea of celibacy (even if they were married) became strident misogynists in an effort to curb their own natural instincts. They permitted themselves to be dedicated to one woman, or a few, while condemning women in general and marriage to them in particular. For male ascetics, lust was a constant temptation, so they needed women to be covered and confined, or better still, enclosed. They needed the women around them to be vowed to celibacy so that the women would bear the responsibility of not being attractive to, or attracted to, men.

13.3. Christian Women of the 4th Century

There were an amazing number of female Christian leaders in this period although they were not part of the (well-developed) clerical hierarchy. Each of them contributed to our understanding of how the 4th century church functioned.

Many of these women were widows who had faced the death of their husbands with courage and who were exempt from the necessity to remarry if they had produced a child who survived for three years. This feat also entitled them to inherit wealth and they used these opportunities to forge a new path for themselves, influenced largely by the Egyptian monk St Anthony, via Marcella of Rome.

Theirs was still a largely pre-Christian society. Often their parents and perhaps even their husbands were pagan, which made the task of living with Christian principles something of a juggling act. By 'home-schooling' their children they managed to bring up their children in the way of the Lord and prepared both their sons and daughters for leading roles in the church.[249] Their world was only very recently delivered from persecution and at least Macrina the Elder had suffered persecution, herself. Others, notably Olympias, were persecuted for other, more complex, reasons. Each of them had to negotiate around the expectations of those who were not Christians, even out-right pagans: husbands, family members, emperors and society. They had to be brave enough to speak clearly, with an unwavering, uncompromising voice.

Most of these women had been born to high rank and grew up in an 'aristocratic bubble'.[250] This was the pattern followed: being wealthy they sold property, built a monastery in a holy place, became its abbess and gathered together a following; first from among their own relatives (mother, sisters, daughters) and their female servants. A second wave of female monastics was usually composed of local admirers from among the lower social classes. Some female leaders had many hundreds of nuns under their care whom they loved, even though these ascetics were generally from a lower rung of the highly stratified society. They formed families within their monasteries, even adopting children and having 'spiritual daughters' but they also went to great lengths to support their mothers, siblings and offspring throughout their lives. This dedication to family was obvious despite their preference for celibacy, which was born out of desire for excellence in Christianity, not a rejection of kith and kin.

They embraced voluntary poverty, literally obeying Christ by giving away all that they had. They cared for the poor, especially the poor within the church, and laid aside class distinctions.

At the same time they unselfconsciously dealt with popes, emperors, patriarchs and empresses with honesty and charity and quite naturally engaged in theological discourse at the highest level, contending for their views. It is difficult to image, in today's egalitarian age, how accustomed these women were to aristocratic social and academic life and what power their origins commanded, never more so than when Melania the Elder was imprisoned for helping jailed Egyptian monks, but was released when she revealed her rank.[251] These high-born ascetics might don brown shirts, dissolve their estates and dispose of their fortunes, but they could not disguise their education, erudition and familiarity with genteel ways. Melania the Younger demonstrated this when she became the preferred travelling companion of the Empress Eudocia.

These women were 'mothers in Israel' in that they built up the church with their scholarship, generosity, good deeds and prayers. They were all very intelligent and more highly educated than most other Christian women of the time. Their monastic lives were devoted to study, learning the Biblical languages, and to extreme ascetic practices, without which it was (apparently) impossible to please God. Although some exercised gifts of healing, their good-deeds largely consisted of feeding the poor and building cells and monasteries for poorer monks. Like mother hens, these women gathered men under their wings and prioritised their needs, wants and egos above their own, while also loyally embracing their theologies.

They were a remarkable group of capable, dedicated and scholarly women, even embracing academic tasks in their more mature years and leading others into a life of scholarship and renunciation. The principle that the Scriptures could and should be read in a language people understood can be directly attributed to them; especially to Marcella and Paula. But scholarship promoted scholarly controversy, in which many of them engaged with all guns blazing: the Origenist and Pelagian controversies in particular. Being leaders, abbesses, patriarchs and hierarchs this group and their associates established guidelines that both the Eastern and the Western Church followed for more than a thousand years. One can understand their desire to be fully dedicated to following the Lord, without accepting the lifestyle.

Usually the aristocratic ancestry and money these ladies enjoyed were amassed in the pagan past and lasted only about one century: the 4th-5th century, but it laid a foundation for Medieval monasticism. They were the forerunners of female monasticism and established a pattern that was followed for centuries by women who wished to devote themselves to God.

In the new climate women embraced poverty and celibacy and did not reproduce themselves and eventually their money dwindled, because even monastics have to be fed, and the monasteries crumbled away when the trend waned.

This group appears to have been very intelligent but perhaps only because they had been given the best education available to women. They were emotionally stable, patiently guiding and influencing their male counterparts in a natural and matter-of-fact way, not deviously, but speaking the truth in love. The sub-culture they created was an international community of closely connected pious intellectuals, held together by mature, stalwart matriarchs but led by men with great egos and strong wills. Women's voice in the Church was diminished when these women made choices to remain in the background while feeding and housing men and enabling them to live in the limelight. The motherly women edited men's writings, took care of their health and helped them through their various squabbles with each other.

Over time, the enclosure of women within women's institutions cut them off from the wider community and enabled the pagan world to ignore them. Their extreme asceticism damaged their health and shortened their lives: none more so that St Paula's daughter, St Blaesilla, for whom it was fatal. The glorification of virginity, by everyone, ensured that only virgins and widows would have any formal role in the Church and permanently hampered married women's active participation, making them somewhat of a second class of women.

The many devoted Christian women noted above cannot be blamed for efforts by men, even lowly scribes and copyists, to gradually and deliberately air-brush women out of the landscape of Christian theology and praxis so that their many contributions were almost lost. An interesting study by Ally Kateusz has shown that the earliest accounts of women in ministry are longer but each stage of copying and translation was also a redaction so that each generation of a text became more truncated than the last. This can only be deliberate as misogyny increased in the Church.[252]

Many Church Histories and books on Patristics make no mention of 4th century Christian women, which is why they are so little known, but they are at least half of the story. Where would Jerome have been without St Paula's knowledge of Hebrew and where would Bishops Basil of Caesarea, Gregory of Nyssa and Peter of Sebaste have been without the guidance of St Macrina the Younger and where would Augustine of Hippo have been but for the years of devoted prayers and sound common sense of St Monica? These women were leaders in every sense of the word.

Bibliography
Primary Sources
Apostolic Constitutions
Epistle of Barnabas, in A. Louth (ed), M. Staniforth (trans.), Early Christian Writings (London: Penguin, 1968/1987)
Eusebius, *Historia Ecclesia (A.Louth (ed), G.A.Williamson (trans) (Harmondsworth: Penguiiiiiin, 19965/1990).*
Evagrius Scholasticus, *Historia Ecclesiastica A.D. 431 to A.D.594,* M. Whitby (trans.)
(Liverpool: Liverpool UP, 2000).
Protevangelium of James
Sozomen, *Ecclesiastical History,* 324 to 440 A.D., Edward Walford (trans.) (London: H. G. Bohn, 1855).
Tertullian, *Concerning Baptism,* 7.1.
Tertullian, *On the Veiling of Virgins* 9, online.
The Confessions of St Augustine , Henry Chadwick (trans.) (Oxford: Oxford UP, 1991).
'The Acts of Paul and Thecla', Jeremiah Jones (trans. c.1700), https://www.pbs.org/wgbh/pages/frontline/shows/religion/maps/primary/thecla.html [1]
Palladius, *The Lausiac History,*
Pope Gelasius I, *Epistola 14* of
Letters of St. Paulinus of Nola, P. G. Walsh (trans.), (N.Y.: Newman, 1967), 2.125-33.
Letter 46 Paula and Eustochium to Marcella, although attributed to Jerome.
https://www.digital.library.upenn.edu/women/paula/letter/letter.html *Testamentum Domini* 1.19. 23.
Papias of Hierapolis in Eusebius *H.E.*
Pliny's letter to Trajan X. 65, 66.
Reference Works

---

1.   https://www.pbs.org/wgbh/pages/frontline/shows/religion/maps/primary/theclas.html

Augustine Through the Ages an Encyclopedia, Fitzgerald A. and C. Cavadini (eds), (Eerdmans, 1999).

Documents of the Christian Church, 2nd ed.
Henry Bettenson (ed), (London: Oxford University Press, 1968).

Oxford Dictionary of the Christian Church Cross, F. L. and E. A. Livingstone (eds), (London: Oxford University Press, 1992).

Oxford Illustrated History of Christianity ,
John McManners
(Oxford and N.Y.: OUP, 1990).

The New Bible Commentary ,
F. Davidson (ed.)
(IVF: London, 1953/1959/1994).

The Oxford Dictionary of Saints 3rd ed.
David Farmer (ed.), (N.Y. and Oxford: Oxford University Press, 1992).

The New Bible Dictionary 3rd ed., I. H. Marshall et al. (eds), (Leicester: IVP, 1996).

Secondary Sources

Alexander, David and Pat (eds), *Lion Handbook to the Bible* (Lion Publishing,: Oxford, U. K., 1973, 1983).

Alikin, Valeriy A., *The Earliest Hisory of the Chrtistian Gathering: Origin, Development And Content of the Chtristian Gathering in the First to Third Centiuries* (Leiden and Boston: Brill, 2010).

Bagatti, Bellarmino OFM (Eugene Hoade OFM, trans.), The Church from the Circumcision: History and Archaeology of the Judaeo-Christians (Jerusalem: Franciscan Printing Press, 1971/1984/ 2004).

Bauckham, Richard, *Jesus and the Eyewitnesses: The Gospels as Eyewitness Testimony* 2nd ed. *(Grand Rapids, MI: Eerdmans, 2006/ 2017).*

Barnes, Timothy D., *Early Christian Hagiography and Roman History* (Tüubingen: Mohr Siebeck, 2010).

Barnett, Paul. *Jesus & the Rise of Early Christianity* (Downes Grove, ILL:IVP, 1999).

Beard, Mary, John North and Simon Price, *Religions of Rome Vol. 2 , A Sourcebook* (Cambridge University Press, 1958).

Brown, Peter, *Through the Eye of a Needle: Wealth, The Fall of Rome and the Making of Christianity in the West, 359-550 A.D.* (Princeton: Princeton UP, 2012).

Bruce, F. F. *The Spreading Flame* (Paternoster Press, 1958/1962).

Campbell, Deslee, 'The Iconography of Women: A Study of Byzantium and the Byzantine-influenced Western Mediterranean, AD 395-1204'. Thesis for the University of Sydney, 2007.

Cameron, Averil, *The Mediterranean World in Late Antiquity A.D. 395-00* (London and N.Y,: Routledge, 1993).

Cameron, A., 'The Exposure of Children and Greek Ethics', *Classical Review* 46.3 (1932), 105-114

Chapple, Allan, 'Getting Romans to the Right Romans,' *Tyndale Bulletin 62.2 (2011)*

Charlesworth, J. H. (ed), *Jesus and Temple* (Minneapolis, MN: Fortress Press, 1992)

Clark, Elizabeth A., *Jerome, Chrysostom and Friends* (N.Y.: Edwin Mellen Press, 1979).

Cohick, Lynn H. and Amy Brown Hughes, *Christian Women of the Patristic World* (Grand Rapids, MI: Baker Academic, 2017).

Davis, Stephen J., *The Cult of St Thecla: A Tradition of Women's Piety in Late Antiquity* (Oxford University Press, 2001).

Dowley, Tim (ed.), *The History of Christianity : A Lion Handbook* (Oxford: Lion, 1977).

Drinkwater, John and Hugh Elton (eds), *Fifth Century Gaul: a Crisis of Identity* (Cambridge and N.Y.: CUP, 1992).

Dunn, J. D. G., 'Was Christianity A Monotheistic Faith From the Beginning?', *Scottish Journal of Theology* 35 (1988), 303-336

Eisen, Ute, *Women Officeholders in Early Christianity: Epigraphical and Literary Studies* (*a translation from the German*)
(Collegeville: Liturgical Press, 2000).

Foster, John, *After the Apostles: Missionary Preaching in the First Three Centuries*
(SCM, 1961).

Filson, Floyd V., *'The Significance of the Early House Churches',* Journal of Biblical Lierature 58.2 (1939).

García, Jesus, *Magdala Project: A First Centiury Discoverty for the People of the Third Milenium, (Gospa Arts S. L. 2016)*

Holum, Kenneth G., *Theodosian Empresses: Women and Imperial Dominion in Late Antiquity (Berkeley, L.A. and London, 1982).*

Hurtado, Larry, *One Lord: Early Christian Devotion and Ancient Jewish Monotheism* (Philadelphia: Fortress, 1988).

Hurtado, Larry, 'Pre 70 CE Jewish Opposition to Christ Devotion,' *Journal of Theological Studies* 50.1 (Apr. 1999), *35-58.*

Jensen, Robin M., *Understanding Early Christian Art, (London/ N.Y,: Routledge, 2000/2002/2007).*

Kateusz, Ally, *Mary and Early Christian Women: Hidden Leadership* (Palgrave Macmillan, 2019).

Kraeling Carl H., 'The excavations at Dura-Europos: conducted by Yale University and the French Academy of Letters, Final Report 8 Part 2, The Christian building,' New Haven: Dura-Europos Publications,
New York, 1967.

Liang, Stefana Dan, *Retrieving History:* Memory and Identity Formation in the Early Church
(Grand Rapids, NI: Baker Academic,2017).

Madigan, Kevin and Caroline Osiek (eds and trans.), *Ordained Women in the Early Church: A Documentary History (Baltimore: John Hopkins University Press, 2005).*

Miller, Patricia Cox, *Women in Early Christianity; Translations from Greek Texts* (Washington, D.C.: Catholic University of America Press, 2005).

Murphy, Francis X., 'Melania the Elder: A Biographical Note', *Traditio* 5 (1947), 59-77.

Musurillo, H., *The Acts of the Christian Martyrs (Oxford, 1972).*

Pederson, Rena, *The Lost Apostle* (San Francisco: Jossey-Bass, 2006).

Plant, Ian Michael (ed.), *Women Writers of Ancient Greece and Rome: An Anthology* (London: University of Oklahoma Press, 2004).

Rainbow, Paul A., 'Jewish Monotheism as the Matrix for New Testament Christology: A Review Article', *Novum Testamentum* 33.1 (1991), 78-91.

Richards, E. Randolph, *Paul and First-Century Letter Writing: Composition and Collection* (Downers Grove, IVP, 2004).

Ristine, Jennifer, *Mary Magdalene: Insights Froim Ancient Magdala* (Jerusalem, Beit Jala, 2018).

Shelley, Bruce, *Church History in Plain Language, (Dallas, London, Vancouver, Melbourne: Word Publishing, 1982/1996).*

Swan, Laura, *The Forgotten Desert Mothers: Sayings, Lives and Storeys of Early Christian Women (Mahwah: Paulinist Press, 2000).*

Swidler, L. and A. (eds), *Women Priests* (NY: Paulist Press, 1977).

Taylor, Sherwood F., 'St. Jerome and Vitamin A', *Nature* 154 (Dec. 23, 1944).

Torjesen, Karen Jo, *When Women Were Priests (San Francisco: Harper Collins, 1995).*

Tucker, Ruth A., *Extraordinary Women of Christian History* (Grand Rapids: Baker Books, 2016).

van Hook, La Rue, 'The Exposure of Infants at Athens,' *Transactions and Proceedings of the American Philological Association* 51 (1920), 134-145.

Wilder, Terry L., 'Phoebe, the Letter-Carrier of Romans, and the Impact of Her Role on Biblical Theology,' *Southwestern Journal of Theology, 56.1. (2013), 43-51.*

Wilson-Kastner, P. et.al. (eds), *A Lost Tradition: Women Writers of the Early Church* (Washington D.C.: University Press of America, 1981).

Electronic Sources

'Augustine of Hippo', Religionfacts, Internet Encyclopedia of Philosophy, 'Augustine (354-430 CE),' Part 3.

'Basil the Elder', NewAdvent, www.newadvent.org/cathen/ 02330b.htm [2]

Bowser, Samantha, 'Modern Judaism at Dura-Europos', http:/www.academia.edu/3530124/Modern-Judaism-at-Dura-Europos

Castellano, Daniel J., (Part I-II, 2009, Part III 2013, Part IV 2019), *Origen and Origenism,* I.1,www.arcaneknowledge.org/ catholic.origen.htm.

Catholic Online, 'Saint Melania the Elder', https://www.catholic.org/saints/saint.php?saint_id=5058 [3]

'Cerula and Bitalia – Women Bishops? – Women Deacons', Wijngaards Institute for Catholic Research http://www.womendeacons.org/cerula-and-bitalia/ [4]

Chapple, Allan, 'Getting Romans to the Right Romans,' www. Tyndale.cam.aqc.uk/Tyndale-Bulletin

Clark, Elizabeth A., *'Melania, Elder', in* A. Gerontius, *Vita Sanctae Melania Junioris* (Life of Melania the Younger) in Monastic Matrix, 'Melania the Younger', https://www.monasticmatrix.osu.edu/vitae/ melania-younger

---

2.   http://www.newadvent.org/cathen/02330b.htm

3.   https://www.catholic.org/saints/saint.php?saint_id=5058

4.   http://www.womendeacons.org/cerula-and-bitalia/

Covington, Richard, 'Mary Magdalene was None of the Things a Pope Claimed', U.S. News and World Report, 25/1/2008. https://www.usnews.com/news/religion/articles/2008/01/25/ mary-magdalene-was-none-[5]of-the-things-a-pope-claimed [6]

Dorman, Marianne Dorman, "St Jerome and the Holy Women of Rome" http//mariannedorman.homestead.com/ JeromeandPaula.html

Ekstrand, D. W., 'Literacy in the Greco-Roman World', http://www.thetransformedsoul.com/aditional-studies/ miscellaneous-studies/-worship-in-the-early-church [7]

Ekstrand, D.W., 'Literacy in the Roman World', https://quod.lib.uich/edu.cgi/t/ text-idc=acas:cc=acls:view=loc:idno...

Eternal Word Television Network, 'St Olympias, Widow - 368-410', https://www.ewtn.com/library/MARY/OLYMPIAS.htm [8]

Ford, Dr David C., 'St. Olympia the Deaconess, Confidante of St. John Chrysostom', https://saintolympiaorthodoxchurch.org/ index.php/resources/9-st-olympia-the-deaconess [9]

'Holy Woman Olympias (Olympiada) the Deaconess of Constantinople', by the Orthodox Church of America. https://oca.org/saints/lives/2013/07/25/102087-holy-woman- olympias-olympiada-the-[10]deaconess-of-constantinople [11]

---

5.   https://www.usnews.com/news/religion/articles/2008/01/25/mary-magdalene-was-none-of-the-things-a-pope-claimed

6.   https://www.usnews.com/news/religion/articles/2008/01/25/mary-magdalene-was-none-of-the-things-a-pope-claimed

7.   http://www.thetransformedsoul.com/aditional-studies/miscellaneous-studies/-worship-in-the-early-church

8.   https://www.ewtn.com/library/MARY/OLYMPIAS.htm

9.   https://saintolympiaorthodoxchurch.org/index.php/resources/9-st-olympia-the-deaconess

Kroeger, Catherine, 'The Neglected History of Women in the Early Church'. https://christianhistoryinstitute.org/magazine/article/women-in-the-early-church [12]

Religionfacts, 'St Augustine of Hippo', www.religionfacts.com/augustine [13]

'Meletius of Antioch', Encyclopedia, H. Leclercq, Catholic Answers. https://catholic.com/encyclopedia/meletus-of-antioch [14]

Melkite Greek Catholic Church: Eparchy of Newton, 'Orders of Widows and Deaconesses https://melkite.org/faith/orders-of-widows-and-deaconesses [15]

National Catholic Reporter 49.6 (Jan. 4, 2013), 'From heads of house churches to presbyters: early Christian women leaders' http://ncronline.org/ [16]

Mirus, Jeff, 'St. Ambrose's impact on St. Augustine: Excerpts from *The Confessions*', https://www.catholicculture.org/commentary/articles.cfm?id=703 [17]

Palladius, *The Lausiac History*, Chapter LVL. 1. www.tertullian.org/fathers/palladius_lausiac_02_text_htm#C46 [18]

'Paula the elder' https://epistolae.ctl.columbia.edu/woman/34.html

---

10.   https://oca.org/saints/lives/2013/07/25/102087-holy-woman-olympias-olympiada-the-deaconess-of-constantinople

11.   https://oca.org/saints/lives/2013/07/25/102087-holy-woman-olympias-olympiada-the-deaconess-of-constantinople

12.   https://christianhistoryinstitute.org/magazine/article/women-in-the-early-church

13.   http://www.religionfacts.com/augustine

14.   https://catholic.com/encyclopedia/meletus-of-antioch

15.   https://melkite.org/faith/orders-of-widows-and-deaconesses

16.   http://ncronline.org/

17.   https://www.catholicculture.org/commentary/articles.cfm?id-703

18.   http://www.tertullian.org/fathers/palladius_lausiac_02_text_htm#C46

'Paulinus, Bishop Eustathian Party at Antioch,' *Dictionary of Early Christian Biography* https://www.studylight.org/dictionaries/hwd/p/paulinus-bishop-eustathian-party-at-antioch.html.

'Saint Nonna Mother of Saint Gregory', httpp://www.johnsanidopoulos.com/2016/08/saint-nonna-of-nazianzus.html

'Ss Emmelia, Nonna and Anthousa – Mothers of three...' https://www.johnsanidooulos.com/2016/02/saints-emmelia-nonna-and-Anthousa.html [19]

'St Jerome', Christian Song Lyrics. https://www.Christian-songlyrics.net/20/09/st-jerome-html

The Editors of Encyclopaedia Britannica, 'Eudocia'. https://www.britannica.com/biography/Eudocia

The Orthodox Church in America, 'Holy Woman Olympias (Olympiada) the Deaconess of Constantinople', https://oca.org/saints/lives/2013/07/25/102087-holy-woman-olympias-the-deaconess-of-[20]constantinople [21]

---

19.   https://www.johnsanidooulos.com/2016/02/saints-emmelia-nonna-and-Anthousa.html

20.   https://oca.org/saints/lives/2013/07/25/102087-holy-woan-olympias-the-deaconess-pf-comstantinople

21.   https://oca.org/saints/lives/2013/07/25/102087-holy-woan-olympias-the-deaconess-pf-comstantinople

ENDNOTES

1 Ally Kateusz, *Mary and Early Christian Women* (Palgrave MacMillan, 2019).

2 This file is licensed under the Creative Commons Attribution 2.9 Generic license.

3 Jesus García, *Magdala Project: A First Centuary Discovery for the People of the Third Millenium,* (Gospa Arts S. L. 2016) p. 184.

4 Richard Covington, 'Mary Magdalene was None of the Things a Pope Claimed', U.S. News and World Report, 25/1/2008.
https://www.usnews.com/news/religion/articles/2008/01/25/
mary-magdalene-was-none-[22]of-the-things-a-pope-claimed [23] [Accessed 9/7/2018].

5 Rena Pederson, *The Lost Apostle* (hereafter *Lost Apostle*) (San Francisco: Jossey-Bass, 2006), pp.50-51 and f/n. 6, citing John Rivera, 'Scholars set the record straight on Mary Magdalene', *Baltimore Sun*, April 19, 2003.

6 Dan Bahat, 'Second Temple', in J. H. Charlesworth (ed.), *Jesus and Temple: Textual and Archaeological Explorations* (Fortress Press, 2014), p. 71.

7 *Ibid.*

8 Jennifer Ristone, *Mary Magdalene: Insights From Ancient Magdala* (Latin Patriarchate Printing Press: Jerusalem, Beit Jala, 2018), p. 69.

9 I. H. Marshall et al. (eds), *The New Bible Dictionary* 3rd ed. (Leicester: IVP, 1996), *s.v.,* Mary.4 agrees although stating that Mary Cleopas in Luke 24:18 was a different person.

10 Such as on the ivory panel c.400 in the Bayerisches Nationalmuseum, Munich.

11 Eusebius, *H.E.*, III. 32, citing Hegessipus.

12 One of the difficulties about terms for women's ministry is that they meant different things in different regions (Syria, Egypt and Rome, for example) and in different centuries.

13 Marshall et al. (eds), *NBD, op.cit., s.v.* Phoebe.

14 Allan Chapple, 'Getting Romans to the Right Romans,' *TB* 62.2 (2011), p.201, f/n. 24 and online: www. Tyndale.cam.aqc.uk/Tyndale-Bulletin [Accessed 2/1/2018].
Randolph Richards, *Paul and First-Century Letter Writing: Composition and Collection* (Downers Grove, IVP, 2004), pp. 163-169.

15 *Ibid.,* p. 211 and f/n. 68, citing Richards, *Paul and First-Century Letter Writing,* pp. 163-69.

16 Chapple, *op.cit.,* p. 213, f/n. 77.

---

22.   https://www.usnews.com/news/religion/articles/2008/01/25/mary-magdalene-was-none-of-the-things-a-pope-claimed

23.   https://www.usnews.com/news/religion/articles/2008/01/25/mary-magdalene-was-none-of-the-things-a-pope-claimed

17 Terry L. Wilder, 'Phoebe, the Letter-Carrier of Romans, and the Impact of Her Role on Biblical Theology,' *SJT*, 56.1. (2013), pp. 44-5.

18 Elizabeth Schüssler Fiorenza, 'The Apostleship of Women in Early Christianity', in L. & A. Swidler, *Women Priests* (NY: Paulist Press, 1977), p. 17.

19 F. Davidson (ed.), *The New Bible Commentary* (IVF: London, 1953/1959/1994), *s.v.* , The Epistle to the Romans: Introduction.

20 If this Rufus was the brother of Alexander his mother was the wife of Simon of Cyrene, the man who was compelled to carry Christ's cross (Mk. 15:21).

21 Romans 16:5; 16:8; 16:9 and 16:17.

22 Torjesen, Karen Jo, *When Women Were Priests* (San Francisco, Harper, 1995) , p. 33.

23 *Ibid*

24 Date accepted by H. Musurillo, *The Acts of the Christian Martyrs* (Oxford, 1972), p. xxvii.

25 *Ibid.,* p. xxvi.

26 Patricia Wilson-Kastner (trans.), in P. Wilson-Kastner et.al. (eds), *A Lost Tradition: Women Writers of the Early Church* (hereafter *Lost Tradition*) (Washington D.C.: University Press of America, 1981), p. 1.

27 Slaves were not usually permitted to marry and their children were born slaves.

28 *Ibid*, pp. 109-117.

29 Stephen J. Davis, *The Cult of St Thecla: A Tradition of Women's Piety in Late Antiquity* (Oxford UP, 2001), p. 4.

30 Jeremiah Jones (trans. c Elizabeth Schüssler Fiorenza, 'The Apostleship of Women in Early Christianity, in L. and A. Swidler, *Women Priests* (NY: Paulist Press, 1977), p. 17.

'The Acts of Paul and Thecla'

https://www.pbs.org/wgbh/pages/frontline/shows/religion/maps/primary/theclas.html [24]

31 Pederson, *Lost Apostle, op.cit.*, pp. 1-3.

32 Lynn H. Cohick and Amy Brown Hughes, *Christian Women of the Patristic World* (Baker, 2017) includes a circular wall-plaque (Fig. 1.2), an ivory panel (one of a series about Thekla) (Fig. 1.3) and a wall-painting in a cave (Fig. 1.1).

33 "Discovered in 1906 in the Cave of St. Thecla and St. Paul on the northern slope of Bülbül Dag, above the ruins of ancient Ephesus. They both have the same height and are therefore iconographically of equal importance. They both have their right hands raised in teaching gesture and are therefore iconographically of equal authority. But while the eyes and upraised hand of Paul are untouched, some later person scratched out the eyes and erased the upraised hand of Thecla. An earlier

---

24.   https://www.pbs.org/wgbh/pages/frontline/shows/religion/maps/primary/theclas.html

image in which Thecla and Paul were equally authoritative apostolic figures has been replaced by one in which the male is apostolic and authoritative and the female is blinded and silenced." (reference: John Dominic Crossan: *In Search of Paul*).

34 Pederson, *Lost Apostle, op.cit.*, p. 70 citing J. D. Crossan and J. L. Reed, *In Search of Paul* (2004).

35 "*Cyprian, Eusebius, Epiphanius, Augustine, Gregory Nazianzus, John Chrysostom, and Severus Sulpitius*", *ibid.*, p. 68.

36 *The Acts of Paul and Thekla, 6.*

37 *Ibid.*

38 *Ibid.*, 12.

39 *Ibid.* The illustration in Plate 4.2 is in the public domain.

40 Cohick and Hughes, *op.cit.*, pp. 24-25.

41 Floyd V. Filson, '*The Significance of the Early House Churches*', *JBL* 58.2 (1939), p. 111.

42 Marshall et al (eds.), *NBD, op.cit., s.v.*, Gaius.

43 David and Pat Alexander (eds), *Lion Handbook to the Bible*, (Lion Publishing: Oxford UK, 1973/1983), p. 625. Marshall et al (eds), *NBD, op.cit., s.v.*, Apphia.

44 So identified by Barnett, *op.cit.*, p. 198. As James and his group were not present at the prayer meeting they may have met elsewhere, even in another house-church, as there were thousands of Judaeo-Chrsitians in Jerusalem.

45 Some think that the 'upper roon' was in John-Mark's mother's house, e,g., John Foster, *After the Apostles: Missionary Preaching in the First Three Centuries* (SCM, 1961), p. 40. Some think that Mark was the youth who fled naked at Jesus' arrest (Mk. 14:51).

46 Filson, *op.cit.*, p.109.

47 In different periods of persecution different proofs of loyalty to the emperor were required, for example, signing certificates of loyalty, libations of wine and burning incense to the emperor's image, invoking the gods, tasting the sacrifices and cursing Christ.

48 Mary Beard, John North and Simon Price, *Religions of Rome Vol. 2 , A Sourcebook* (Cambridge University Press, 1958), p. 165.

49 As James and his group were not present at the prayer meeting they may have met elsewhere, probably sin another house-church.

50 For Mark as Peter's scribe, Papias of Hierapolis and Eusebius *H.E.* III.39.14, see Paul Barnett, (*Jesus & the Rise of Early Christianity* (Downes Grove, ILL:IVP, 1999), p. 392.

Richard Bauckham argues that the two collaborated on it, in *Jesus and the Eyewitnesses: The Gospels as Eyewitness Testimony* 2nd ed. (hereafter *Eyewitnesses*) (Grand Rapids, MI: Eerdmans, 2006/2017).

51 Some Romans deliberately purchased literate slaves or had them educated as business assistants, see D. W. Ekstrand, 'Literacy in the Greco-Roman World'
http://www.thetransformedsoul.com/aditional-studies/
miscellaneous-studies/-worship-in-[25]the-early-church [26][Accessed 21/7/2018].

52 D. W. Ekstrand, 'Literacy in the Roman World', [Accessed 7/5/2019]. https://quod.lib.uich/edu.cgi/t/text-idc=acas:cc=acls:view=loc:idno...

53 Ekstrand, 'Literacy in the Greco-Roman World', *op.cit.*, online.

54 Valeriy A. Alikin, *The Earliest History of the Christian Gathering: Origin, Development and Content of the Christian Gathering in the First to Third Centuries (Leiden/Boston: Brill, 2010)*, p. 55.

55 Dura also had temples to many pagan gods as well as the lavishly decorated synagogue.

56 Drawn by Udimu, redrawn (2006) from Carl H. Kraeling with a contribution by C. Bradford Welles: The excavations at Dura-Europos: conducted by Yale University and the French Academy of Letters, Final Report 8 Part 2, The Christian building, New Haven: Dura-Europos Publications, New York, 1967, fig. 1, p. 4. Republished under the terms of the GNU Free Documentation License, Version 1.2.

57 Tertullian, *Concerning Baptism*, 7.1. and Souter's trans. f/n 33, specified olive oil and that the precedent was Moses' anointing of Aaron and his sons, Ex. 3030; Lev.8.12.

58 Robin M. Jensen, *Early Christian Art* (London/N.Y,: Routledge, 2000/2002/2007), p. 87.

59 Samantha Bowser, 'Modern Judaism at Dura-Europos', [Accessed 1/1/2020]. http:/www.academia.edu/3530124/Modern-Judaism-at-Dura-Europos

60 Bellarmino Bagatti (Eugene Hoade, trans.), *The Church from the Circumcision: History and Archaeology of the Judaeo-Christians* (Jerusalem, 1971/1984/2004), p. 26.

61 For advanced discussions of the issue of the early worship of Christ see Larry Hurtado, *One Lord: Early Christian Devotion and Ancient Jewish Monotheism* (Philadelphia: Fortress, 1988) and Hurtado, 'Pre 70 CE Jewish Opposition to Christ Devotion,' *op.cit.,* pp. 35-58. See also J. D. G. Dunn, 'Was Christianity A Monotheistic Faith From the Beginning?', *Scottish JT* 35 (1988), pp. 303-336 and Paul A. Rainbow, 'Jewish Monotheism as the Matrix for New Testament Christology: A Review Article', *NT* 33.1 (1991), pp. 78-91.

62 Torjesen, *op.cit.*, p. 40.

63 Filson, *op.cit.,* p. 110.

64 Torjesen, *op.cit.,* p. 166.

---

25.   http://www.thetransformedsoul.com/aditional-studies/miscellaneous-studies/-worship-in-the-early-church

26.   http://www.thetransformedsoul.com/aditional-studies/miscellaneous-studies/-worship-in-the-early-church

65 Tertullian, *Concerning Baptism* 17, *op.cit.*, online 66 Torjesen, *op.cit.*, p. 169.

67 Cross and Livingstone (eds), *ODCC, op.cit., s.v.*, Tertullian, Quintus Septimus Florens.

68 Torjesen, *op.cit.*, p. 172.

69 It seems that the role of presbyter did not evolve as early as those of deacon (one who serves) and bishop (in Greek *epi skopos* one who over looks, i.e., an overseer) but 'presbyter' was a common term in the Pastoral Epistles.

70 Ruth A. Tucker, *Extraordinary Women of Christian History* (hereafter *Women*) (Grand Rapids: Baker Books, 2016), p. 9.

71 *Ibid.*, p. 10.

72 Cohick and Hughes, *op.cit.*, p. 197.

73 Cross and Livingstone (ed.), *ODCC, op.cit., s.v.* Marcella, St 74 Religionfacts, 'St Augustine of Hippo', www.religionfacts.com/augustine [Accessed 19/2/2019].

75 This was a mixture of ideas which rejected the Old Testament and God and incorporated dualism, asceticism, and determinism. Its founder, Mani, had been martyred in Persia c. 267. Religionfacts, 'Augustine of Hippo', *op.cit.*, online. Bruce Shelley, *Church History in Plain Language,* (Dallas, London, Vancouver, Melbourne: Word Publishing, 1982/1996), pp. 125-127.

76 Jeff Mirus, 'St. Ambrose's impact on St. Augustine: Excerpts from *The Confessions*', https://www.catholicculture.org/commentary/articles.cfm?id=703 [27][Accessed 19/2/2018]. A modern translation of *The Confessions of St Augustine* by Henry Chadwick is available (Oxford: Oxford UP, 1991).

77 *Ibid.*, citing from Book 5 of Augustin's *Confessions*. Mirus, 'St. Ambrose's impact on St. August bk 5, *op.cit.*

78 *Ibid.*, citing Book 6.

79 Religionfacts, 'Augustine of Hippo', *op.cit.*, online.

80 Augustine, *Confessions*, VI.2.2.

81 *Ibid.*, citing Gerald Bonner, St Augustine of Hippo: Life and Controversies (3rd edition) (Canterbury Press Norwich, 2002), p. 38; Cohick and Hughes, *op.cit.*, p. 180.

82 Mirus, *op.cit.*, citing Book 6 of *The Confessions*'.

83 *Ibid.*, citing Book 9.

84 Religionfacts, 'Augustine of Hippo', *op.cit.*, online.

85 Mirus, *op.cit.*, citing Book 9 of ' *The Confessions*'.

86 Internet Encyclopedia of Philosophy, 'Augustine (354-430 CE),' Part 3. https://www.iep.utm.edu/augustin/ [Accessed [28]19/2/2019].

87 Religionfacts, 'Augustine of Hippo', *op.cit.*, online; Shelley, *op.cit.*, pp.125-127.

---

27.   https://www.catholicculture.org/commentary/articles.cfm?id-703

28.   https://www.iep.utm.edu/augustin/%5bAccessed

88 Religionfacts, 'Augustine of Hippo', *op.cit.*, online 89 Cohick and Hughes, *op.cit.*, p. 181, f/note 86 and p. 183, f/note 96 for details of English translations.

90 *Ibid.*, p. 181.

91 Cross and Livingstone (eds), *ODCC, op.cit., s.v.* Chrysostom, John, St.. 'Ss Emmelia, Nonna and Anthousa – Mothers of three...' [3/3.2019]. https://www.johnsanidooulos.com/2016/02/saints-emmelia-nonna-and-Anthousa.html [29]

92 Her husband of a twenty days was Nebrius, ex-prefect of Constantinople, and her father was Seleucus, the ex-count. Palladius, *The Lausiac History*, Chapter LVL. 1. Her paternal grandfather was the Praetorian prefect, consul and senator, Ablabius.

www.tertullian.org/fathers/palladius_lausiac_02_text_htm#C46 [30][Accessed 1/1/2019].

Dr David C. Ford, 'St. Olympia the Deaconess, Confidante of St. John Chrysostom',[Accessed 1/1/2019] https://saintolympiaorthodoxchurch.org/index. [31]php/resources/9-st-olympia-the-deaconess

93 Kevin Madigan and Carolyn Osiek (eds and trans) *Ordained Women in the Early Church: A Documentary History* (Baltimore: Johns Hopkins University Press,2005).

385. Palladius, *The Lausiac History*, LVI .1, *op.cit.*, online.

94 *Ibid*

95 Eternal Word Television Network, 'St Olympias, Widow - 368-410', https://www.ewtn.com/library/MARY/OLYMPIAS.htm [32][Accessed 1/1/'19].

96 Madigan and Osiek (eds and trans), *op.cit.* , p. 43.

97 *Ibid.*, p. 82.

98 Palladius, *The Lausiac History*, LVI.1, *op.cit.*, online.

99 Her fellow deaconesses of the Cathedral were Pentadia, Proklia and Salbina. 'Holy Woman Olympias (Olympiada) the Deaconess of Constantinople', by the Orthodox Church of America. https://oca.org/saints/lives/2013/07/25/102087-holy-woman-olympias-[33]olympiada-the-deaconess-of-constantinople [34][Accessed 11/1/2019].

100 Madigan and Osiek (eds and trans), *op.cit.* , p, *op.cit.* , p. 126.

---

29.   https://www.johnsanidooulos.com/2016/02/saints-emmelia-nonna-and-Anthousa.html

30.   http://www.tertullian.org/fathers/palladius_lausiac_02_text_htm#C46

31.   https://saintolympiaorthodoxchurch.org/index

32.   https://www.ewtn.com/library/MARY/OLYMPIAS.htm

33.   https://oca.org/saints/lives/2013/07/25/102087-holy-woman-olympias-olympiada-the-deaconess-of-constantinople

34.   https://oca.org/saints/lives/2013/07/25/102087-holy-woman-olympias-olympiada-the-deaconess-of-constantinople

101 *Ibid.*, p. 44 citing Life of Olympias 6 , translated in Elizabeth A. Clark, *Jerome, Chrysostom and Friends* (N.Y,: Edwin Mellen Press, 1979) , *pp.* 117-119, 145-157

102 *Ibid.*, p. 34.

103 For a text of the anonymous 'Life of Olympia' see Elizabeth A. Clark, *Jerome, Chrysostom and Friends, op.cit.*, pp. 127-42.

104 *Ibid.*

105 Kenneth G. Holum, *Theodosian Empresses: Women and Imperial Dominion in Late Antiquity* (Berkeley, L.A. and London, 1982), p. 143 citing her *Vita*, 8. edited by A-M.

Malingrey, *Jean Chrisostom, Letters à St Olympias* (Paris, 1968).

106 Eternal Word Television Network, 'St Olympias, Widow - 368-410', *op.cit.*, online.

107 *Ibid.*

108 Torjesen, *op.cit.*, p. 109, f/ns. 28; 29 citing F. X. Murphy,'Melania the Younger: A Biographical Note', *Traditio* 5 (1947): 59-77 and Clark, *Jerome, Chrysostom and Friends, op.cit.*, pp. 107-57.

109 Palladious, *The Lausiac History*, LVI. 2, *op.cit.*, online..

110 Eternal Word Television Network, 'St Olympias, Widow - 368-410', *op.cit.*, online.

111 The Orthodox Church in America, 'Holy Woman Olympias (Olympiada) the Deaconess of Constantinople', https://oca.org/saints/lives/2013/07/25/102087-holy-woman-olympias-the-deaconess-of-[35]constantinople [36]

112 Palladius, *The Lausiac History*, LIV and XLI.4, *op.cit.*, online.

113 Cross and Livingstone (eds), *ODCC, op.cit., s.v.* Gregory Thaumaturgus, St.

114 Farmer (ed.), *ODS, op.cit., s.v.,* Macrina the Elder.

115 Cohick and Hughes (eds and trans), *op.cit.*, p. 163, f/n 13. See also NewAdvent, 'Basil the Elder', www.newadvent.org/cathen/02330b.htm [37][Assessed 1/4/'19].

116 Cohick and Hughes (eds and trans), *op.cit.*, p. 163. Laing, *op.cit.*, pp. 141, 144, 147.

117 John McManners, *Oxford Illustrated History of Christianity* (hereafter *OIHC*) (Oxford and N.Y.: OUP, 1990), p. 133.

118 Cohick and Hughes (eds and trans), *op.cit.*, p. 163.

119 Macrina the Younger's most complete biography is by Gerontius.

120 Cohick and Hughes (eds and trans), *op.cit.*, p. 166.

---

35.   https://oca.org/saints/lives/2013/07/25/102087-holy-woan-olympias-the-deaconess-pf-comstantinople

36.   https://oca.org/saints/lives/2013/07/25/102087-holy-woan-olympias-the-deaconess-pf-comstantinople

37.   http://www.newadvent.org/cathen/02330b.htm

121 Stefana Dan Laing, *Retrieving History: Memory and Identity Formation in the Early Church* (Baker Academic: Grand Rapids, 2017), pp. 140-145.

122 Cohick and Hughes (eds and trans), *op.cit.*, p. 163.

123 Cross and Livingstone (eds), *ODCC, op.cit., s.v.* Macrina, St 124 Patricia Wilson-Kastner, 'Introduction', in Wilson-Kastner et al. (eds), *Lost Tradition, op.cit.*, pp. xvii-xviii.

125 At this time in Constantinople deaconesses had to be dedicated to celibacy. Eternal Word Television Network, 'St Olympias, Widow - 368-410', *op.cit.*, online.

126 'Saint Nonna Mother of Saint Gregory', [Accessed/1/2019]. httpp://www.johnsanidopoulos.com/2016/08/saint-nonna-of-nazianzus.html

127 So LIV.1, *op.cit.*, online.

128 *Ibid.* LIV.1.

129 Author and Publisher - Catholic Online, 'Saint Melania the Elder', [Accessed 21/1/2019]. https://www.catholic.org/saints/saint.php?saint_id=5058 [38]

130 Palladius, *The Lausiac History*, LV.3 *op.ci* t., online.

131 Cohick and Hughes (eds and trans), *op.cit.*, pp. 206-07.

132 Francis X. Murphy, 'Melania the Elder: A Biographical Note', *Traditio* 5 (1947), p. 64.

133 Cohick and Hughes (eds and trans), *op.cit.*, p. 204 and p. 205, f/n. 59.

134 *Ibid.*, p. 53

135 Palladius, *The Lausiac History* 46.

136 Author and Publisher Catholic online, 'Saint Melania the Elder, *op.cit.*, online.

137 Palladius, *The Lausiac History*, 9.

138 Patricia Cox Miller, *Women in Early Christianity: Translations From the Greek Texts* (hereafter *Women in Early Christianity*), (Washington, D.C., 2005), pp. 208-09.

139 P. G. Walsh (trans.), *Letters of St. Paulinus of Nola* (N.Y.: Newman, 1967), 2.125-33.

140 Cohick and Hughes (eds and trans), *op.cit.*, p. 135.

141 Francis X. Murphy, 'Melania the Elder: A Biographical Note', *Traditio* 5 (1947), p. 59.

Melania means "blackness" in Greek, Miller, *Women in Early Christianity, op.cit.*, p. 208.

143 Palladius, *The Lousiac History*, LVC. 1, *op.cit.*, online.

144 Miller, *Women in Early Christianity*, citing Palladius, *Lausiac History*, LIV.

145 *Ibid.*

---

38.   https://www.catholic.org/saints/saint.php?saint_id=5058

146 Palladius, *The Lausiac History*, LIV. 6, *op.cit.*, online.

147 Elizabeth A. Clark, '*Melania, Elder*', *in* A. Fitzgerald and C. Cavadini (eds), *Augustine Through the Ages an Encyclopedia* (Eerdmans, 1999).

148 Gerontius, *Vita Sanctae Melania Junioris* (Life of Melania the Younger) in Monastic Matrix, 'Melania the Younger', https://www.monasticmatrix.osu.edu/vitae/melania-younger [Accessed 2/2/2019].

149 Cohick and Hughes (eds and trans), *op.cit.*, p. 198 and f/n. 28.

150 Jerome's *Lettter* 108 records Paula's early life, *Letter* 127 is a Life of Marcella.

151 Cohick and Hughes (eds and trans), *op.cit.*, p. 198.

152 'Paula the elder' https://epistolae.ctl.columbia.edu/woman/34.html *Ibid.*, pp. 199-200, citing Jerome, *Epistle* 108.20.1-7.

153 *Ibid.*, pp. 162-68.

154 'Paula the elder' https://epistolae.ctl.columbia.edu/woman/34.html 155 Cohick and Hughes (eds and trans), *op.cit.*, p. 199.

156 *Ibid.*, p. 192.

157 *Ibid.*, pp. 198-99.

158 Sherwood F. Taylor,'St. Jerome and VitaminA', *Nature* 154 (Dec.23, 1944), p.802.

159 *Letter 46 Paula and Eustochium to Marcella*, although attributed to Jerome. *https://www.digital.library.upenn.edu/women/paula/letter/letter.html[*[39]*Acessed   27/12/2018]*.

160 T. S. M. Mommaerts and D. H. Kelly, 'The Anicii of Gaul and Rome in Fifth Century Gaul: a Crisis of Identity?' in John Drinkwater and Hugh Elton (eds), *Fifth Century Gaul: a Crisis of Identity* (Cambridge and N.Y.: CUP, 1992), pp. 120-21.

161 Cohick and Hughes (eds and trans), *op.cit.*, p. 199.

162 Rader, 'Introduction', in Wilson-Kastner et al., *Lost Tradition, op.cit.*, pp. 4-5.

163 Laura Swan, *The Forgotten Desert Mothers: Sayings, Lives and Storeys of Early Christian Women* (Mahwah: Paulinist Press, 2000), p. 141.

164 The most reliable text of the Vulgate, the *Codex Amiatinus*, was produced in England in one of the great Benedictine monasteries of Wearmouth or Jarrow, under Abbott Ceolfrid, c.716, F. F. Bruce, *The Spreading Flame*, (Paternoster Press, 1958/1962), pp. 414-15.

165 Cohick and Hughes (eds and trans), *op.cit.*, p. 198, referencing Jerome, *Epistle* 22.

166 Ruth A. Tucker, *Extraordinary Women of Christian History* (Baker Books, 2016), p. 11.

167 Palladius, *The Lausiac History* LXII, *op.cit.*, online notes (rather vaguely) that Pammachius was a relative of 'the Melanias'.

---

39.   *https://www.digital.library.upenn.edu/women/paula/letter/letter.html*

168 Tucker , *op.cit.*, p. 11, citing Marianne Dorman, "St Jerome and the Holy Women of Rome" http://mariannedorman.homestead.com/JeromeandPa[40]ula.html

169 'Meletius of Antioch', Encyclopedia, H. Leclercq, Catholic Answers. https://catholic.com/encyclopedia/meletus-of-antioch [41][Accessed 27/6/2020].

170 ' Paulinus, Bishop Eustathian Party at Antioch,' *A Dictionary of Early Christian Biography* https://www.studylight.org/dictionaries/hwd/p/paulinus-bishop-eustathian-party-at-antioch.html. 1911 [Accessed 27/6/2020].

171 'Meletius of Antioch', Encyclopedia, H. Leclercq, Catholic Answers, *op.cit.*, online.

172 *Ibid.*

173 Holum, *op.cit.*, p. 18.

174 'St Jerome', Christian Song Lyrics. https://www.Christian-songlyrics.net/20/09/st-jerome-html.

175 Holum, *op.cit.*, pp. 16-17.

176 Tim Dowley (ed.), *The History of Christianity* (Oxford: Lion, 1977), p. 174.

177 Cross and Livingstone (eds), *ODCC, op.cit., s.v.* Origen.

178 Daniel J. Castellano (Part I-II, 2009, Part III 2013, Part IzV 2019), *Origen and Origenism*, I.1, www.arcaneknowledge.org/catholic.origen.htm.

179 *Ibid.*, I. 2

180 *Ibid.*

181 As a widower, this peace-loving senator became a monk, devoting his money to good works. He died in the Gothic invasion of 410.

182 Castellano, *Origen and Origenism, op.cit.,* I.3.2.

183 Cross and Livingstone (eds), *ODCC, op. cit., s.v.,* Origenism.

184 *Ibid., s.v.,* Pelagius.

185 Nestorius was appointed Patriarch of Constantinople by the emperor Theodosius II from 428 until he was deposed by the Council of Ephesus in 431 before eventually being banished to Upper Egypt where he died c.451.

186 Henry Bettenson (ed.), *Documents of the Christian Church* (London Oxford University Press, 1968), p. 83.

187 Cross and Livingstone (eds), *ODCC, op. cit.,* s.v., Pelagius.

188 Cohick and Hughes, *op.cit.*, p. 209, f/n. 81, citing Elizabeth Clark's 1984 translation of Gerontius, *Vita Melania*, 1. The *Vita* has survived in Greek and Latin but the Greek text is superior, Timothy D. Barnes, *Early Christian Hagiography and Roman History* (Tüubingen: Mohr Siebeck, 2010), p. 249.

189 Palladius, *Lausiac History*, LV.3, *op.cit.*, onluine.

190 Cohick and Hughes (eds and trans), *op.cit.*, p. 209-11.

---

40.   http://mariannedorman.homestead.com/Jeromeand

41.   https://catholic.com/encyclopedia/meletus-of-antioch

191 Peter Brown, *Through the Eye of a Needle: Wealth, The Fall of Rome and the Making of Christianity in the West, 359-550 A.D.* (Princeton: Princeton UP, 2012), pp. 291.-301.

192 Cohick and Hughes (eds and trans), *op.cit.*, p. 212.

193 *Ibid.*, p. 214, citing *On the Crest of Grace*, which Augustine wrote in reply. In fact, Augustine was strongly opposed to Pelagius.

194 "Vita Sanctae Melaniae," Esc. a II 9, fol 103 and 103v, cited by Joyce E. Salisbury, 'Early Christian Virgins on Sexuality and Virginity'. [Accessed 20/6/2020]. https://www.versobooks.com/blogs/3612-early-christian-virgins-on-sex

195 Miller, *Women in Early Christianity*, *op.cit.*, p. 19 citing Gerontius, *Life of Melania the Younger* 42.

196 "Vita Sanctae Melaniae," Esc. a II 9, fol. 109, cited by Joyce E. Salisbury, *op.cit.*, online.

197 *Ibid.*, Esc. a II 9, fol. 108v. cited by Joyce E. Salisbury, *op.cit.*, online.

198 Averil Cameron, *The Mediterranean World in Late Antiquity A.D. 395-600* (hereafter *Mediterran-ean World*) (London and N.Y,: Routledge, 1993), p. 68; Holum, *op.cit.*, pp. 193-94.

199 Joyce Salisbury, *op.cit.*, online.

200 Miller, *Women in Early Christianity*, *op.cit.*, p. 62.

201 Translated by Connolly, 1929 and Strecker, 1971. See also *National Catholic Reporter* 49.6 (Jan. 4, 2013), 'From heads of house churches to presbyters: early Christian women leaders', p. 10, http://ncronline.org/ [42]and in the bibliography.

202 Tertullian, *On the Veiling of Virgins* 9, online.

203 Torjesen, *op.cit.* , p. 114.

204 *Apostolic Constitutions* 8.19-20.

205 Cohick and Hughes (eds and trans), *op.cit.*, Appendix A.

206 *Testamentum Domini* 1.19. 23.

207 *Ibid.*, 2. 19. On female ministry in the Early Church see Ute Eisen, *Women Officeholders in Early Christianity: Epigraphical and Literary Studies* (Collegeville: Liturgical Press, 2000), a translation from the German.

208 See Madigan and Osiek, *op. cit.*, Appendix A and Appendix C.

209 Cross and Livingstone (eds), *ODCC*, *op.cit.*, s.v. Testamentum Domini.

210 Pederson, (*Lost Apostle*), *op.cit.*, p. 84; *Epistle of Barnabas* 19.3; Pliny's letter to Trajan X. 65, 66. It was a crime in *the Justinian Code*, VIII.51.2 so it must have still occurred. See A. Cameron, 'The Exposure of Children and Greek Ethics', *Classical Review* 46.3 (1932), pp. 105-114 and La Rue van Hook, 'The Exposure of Infants at Athens', *Transactions and Proceedings of the American Philological Association* 51 (1920), pp. 134-145.

---

42.   http://ncronline.org/

211 Dr Catherine Kroeger, 'The Neglected History of Women in the Early Church'. https://christianhistoryinstitute.org/magazine/article/women-in-the-early-church [43][Accessed 1/1/'17].

212 Melkite Greek Catholic Church: Eparchy of Newton, 'Orders of Widows and Deaconesses' https://melkite.org/faith/orders-of-widows-and-deaconesses [44][Accessed 22/2/2019].

213 Madigan and Osiek, *op.cit.*, p. 205.

214 Melkite Greek Catholic Church, 'Orders of Widows and Deaconesses', *op.cit.*, online.

215 Miller, *Women in Early Christianity, op.cit.* , p. 65.

216 Bible references for these women: Ex. 15:20-21; Jud. 4:4; Lk. 2:36-38; II Kings 22:14-20.

217 Miller, *Women in Early Christianity, op.cit.*, pp. 64-65 citing *Apostolic Constitutions* 8.19, 1-20, 1-2.

218 Evagrius Scholasticus, *Historia Ecclesiastica A.D. 431 to A.D.594*, M. Whitby (trans.) (Liverpool: Liverpool UP, 2000), I. 22; Sozomen, *Ecclesiastical History*, 324 to 440 A.D., Edward Walford (trans.) (London: H. G. Bohn, 1855), IX.16.

219 Kenneth G. Holum, *Theodosian Empresses: Women and Imperial Dominion in Late Antiquity (London: University of California Press,* 1982), p. 117.

220 This is the patriarch who replaced John Chrysostom after he was banished.

221 Holum, *op.cit.*, pp. 131-132.

222 *Ibid.*, p. 129.

223 *Ibid.*, p. 214, citing *On the Crest of Grace*, which Augustine wrote in reply. In fact, Augustine was strongly opposed to Pelagius.

224 The Editors of *Encyclopaedia Britannica*, 'Eudocia'.

225 John Bagnell Bury, *History of the Later Roman Empire from Arcadius to Irene*, Vol. I (N.Y. Cosoimo, Incorporated (1889/2008), pp. 131-132

226 Catholic Encyclopedia, 'Eudocia' https://www.newadvent.org/cargen/05597ahtm [45][Accessed 13/6/2020].

227 Holum, *op.cit.*, p. 194.

228 Ian Michael Plant (ed.), *Women Writers of Ancient Greece and Rome: An Anthology* (London: University of Oklahoma Press, 2004), p. 198. Pages 198-209 are devoted to Eudocia.

229 Holum, *op.cit.*, p. 219.

230 See 'Cerula and Bitalia – Women Bishops? – Women Deacons', Wijngaards Institute for Catholic Research.

---

43.   https://christianhistoryinstitute.org/magazine/article/women-in-the-early-church

44.   https://melkite.org/faith/orders-of-widows-and-deaconesses

45.   https://www.newadvent.org/cargen/05597ahtm

231 This image is licensed under the Creative Commons Attribution-Share Alike 2.5 Generic license, by Al Mare, 2000.

232 Kevin Madigan and Caroline Osiek in (eds and trans.), *Ordained Women in the Early Church: A Documentary History* (Baltimore: John Hopkins University Press, 2005).

233 *Ibid.*, pp. 169-171 and 191-203.

234 Creative commons

235 Deslee Campbell, 'The Iconography of Women: A Study of Byzantium and the Byzantine-influenced Western Mediterranean, AD 395-1204'. Thesis for the University of Sydney, 2007, p. 54.

236 *Ibid.*, pp. 380-431 and Plates 4.ii.10 to 27.

237 *Ibid.*, pp. 532-536 and Plates 4.v.19 to 21.

238 Tertullian, *Concerning Baptism* 17, *op.cit.*, online 239 *Epistola* 14 of Pope Gelasius I.

240 Dominik Matus, [46]2017.This file is licensed under the Creative Commons Attribution-Share Alike 4.0 International license.

241 Joyce Salisbury, *op.cit.,* online.

242 Madigan and Osiek, *op.cit.* , Appendix A.

243 Irenaeus, *Against Heresies* and Eusebius, *E H.*, III.20 and 23 and 31.

244 Jennifer Ristine, *Mary Magdalene: Insights From Ancient Magdala* (Jerusalem, Beit Jala, 2018), pp. 100-101.

245 Eusebius, *E.H.* III. 37.1.

246 *Ibid.*, III. 31, quoting Polycrates c.190 AD.

247 Eusebius, *H E.*, III.35

248 Also called the *Protevangelium of James*. Various translations are readily available on the net.

249 Pederson, *Lost Aposte, op.cit.*, p. 85.

250 So Cohick and Hughes (eds and trans), *op.cit.*, p. 212.

251 Another example was when Melania the Elder intervened to prevent St Augustine of Hippo from signing a document, described in Cohick and Hughes (eds and trans), *ibid.*, pp. 211-213..

252 Ally Kateusz, *Mary and Early Christian Women, op.cit.,* (2019).

About the Author

About the Author

Dr Deslee Campbell, a retired educational psychologist and teacher, is a prolific writer of both fiction and works concerned with history, religion and archaeology. She is particularly interested in art, artefacts and architecture as pathways towards understanding the past. Her doctoral thesis from the University of Sydney is entitled "The Iconography of Women: A Study of Byzantium and the Byzantine-influenced Mediterranean, A.D. 395-1204."

Read more at https://www.youtube.com/@synagogueandchurch911.

www.ingramcontent.com/pod-product-compliance
Lightning Source LLC
Chambersburg PA
CBHW031157160726
47992CB00006B/2480